IF ONLY IT HADN'T RAINED

A MEMOIR OF FORCED LABOUR IN THE SECOND WORLD WAR

BY THE SAME AUTHOR:

The Hazelnut Grove

IF ONLY IT HADN'T RAINED

A MEMOIR OF FORCED LABOUR IN THE SECOND WORLD WAR

PAULA READ

Copyright © 2023 Paula Read

The moral right of the author has been asserted.

Apart from any fair dealing for the purposes of research or private study, or criticism or review, as permitted under the Copyright, Designs and Patents Act 1988, this publication may only be reproduced, stored or transmitted, in any form or by any means, with the prior permission in writing of the publishers, or in the case of reprographic reproduction in accordance with the terms of licences issued by the Copyright Licensing Agency. Enquiries concerning reproduction outside those terms should be sent to the publishers.

Matador
Unit E2 Airfield Business Park,
Harrison Road, Market Harborough,
Leicestershire. LE16 7UL
Tel: 0116 2792299
Email: books@troubador.co.uk
Web: www.troubador.co.uk/matador
Twitter: @matadorbooks

ISBN 978 1803136 653

British Library Cataloguing in Publication Data.
A catalogue record for this book is available from the British Library.

Printed and bound in Great Britain by 4edge Limited
Typeset in 12pt Adobe Garamond Pro by Troubador Publishing Ltd, Leicester, UK

Matador is an imprint of Troubador Publishing Ltd

Pour Papa

'Those who died, and those who survived, deserve all the sympathy of the living, but can you go on screaming for vengeance? The rivers renew themselves; nature changes its finery many times and we humans are replaced by new generations. Should we demand of the young that they should take charge of our moral legacy? No, I don't think so. But they should know how to learn from our sufferings and also, it has to be said, from our mistakes.'

Roland Chopard

ACKNOWLEDGEMENTS

Annie and Paula would like to thank Stephen Walton, Senior Curator, Second World War & Mid-20th Century, at the Imperial War Museum, Duxford, for being such a helpful and enthusiastic guardian of Roland Chopard's writings and other artefacts, gathered under the title 'The Chopard Archive' (https://www.iwm.org.uk/research/research-facilities).

Our heartfelt thanks go to the Mayor of Lacapelle-Biron, Nadine Lafon, and to the Association Mémoire Vive, the Living Memory Association, for the generosity of their response to our inquiries. Without the Association's film, *La Rafle au Cœur*, produced by Bernard Semerjian, Jacques Augié and Myriam Semerjian, it would not have been possible to depict the events of that day in May with such immediacy and emotion. We appreciate their enormous skills in making this film. In particular, we would like to thank Marie-Claire Caumières for her considerable help, and for the moving words about her father Raoul Marmié, who was taken by the Germans and who never returned.

Our thanks go also to Annie's husband Nathaniel who was, unwittingly, the initiator of the whole project, and to brother Alexandre for his help in clarifying certain passages for translation into English, and to niece Delphine for the time and effort spent on careful proof-reading of the French version of Roland's memoir. We are also very grateful to Jérôme Duveau for his evocative cover design.

And finally, Annie would like to thank Paula to whom she is eternally grateful. She was moved by Paula's reaction to Roland's story and impressed by her determination and willingness to make it into a more rounded account. In bringing Roland to life, Paula enables everyone to know the man, not just the prisoner of war. Annie believes this book offers a kind of atonement to her father. His story is no longer hidden.

Paula would like to thank her family, husband Hans, daughter Lily and son Roland, for their continuing enthusiastic support, their patience and forbearance, and not least, for their fierce editing skills.

Mostly, however, Paula would like to thank Annie for introducing her to the remarkable writings of Roland Chopard. She feels privileged.

CONTENTS

Acknowledgements	ix
Introduction	xiii
'Où est Rol?'	1
Roland, das Reich, Resistance	18
The Raid on Lacapelle-Biron	29
The Capture	46
The Waiting Ends	61
The Normandy Landings, D-Day 6 June 1944	76
Dachau	88
The Hangings	101
Eisenach	107
The Aeroplanes are Coming	118
The Era of Bestiality	135
Buchenwald	147
Will We Make It?	167
Coming Home	171
The Return	175

INTRODUCTION

In the central square of Lacapelle-Biron stands a monument to the memory of those men from the village arrested and deported on 21 May 1944.

01. AHMED Mustapha*
02. AMADIEU Raymond*
03. AUGIÉ Abel*
04. AZNAR François
05. BALES Etienne
06. BARAS Arthur*
07. BARAS Léopold
08. BARAS Louis
09. BORD Roger
10. BOULLE Noël
11. BUGIER Gilbert*
12. BUGIER René*
13. BULIT André
14. CAMINADE Jean
15. CAUMIÈRES Raymond*
16. CHRÉTIEN Hubert
17. CHRÉTIEN Jean-Claude
18. DANÉ Roger
19. DA SOUZA Mario
20. DELAYRE Hubert*
21. DELAYRE Louis*
22. DELORENZI Auguste*
23. FAGEOL Roger*
24. FAVARETTE Ernesto*
25. GENESTE Pierre*
26. IMBERMON Pedro
27. JAMBOU Roland*
28. JUGE Pierre*
29. LAGARRIGUE Jean*
30. MARCENAT Léopold*
31. MARMIÉ Raoul*
32. MARTY Paul
33. MERDINGER Bernard
34. MIQUEL François*
35. PEREIRA Acacio
36. PERICOLI Jean
37. PICHET André
38. PORTES Paul*
39. POUJADE Jean
40. RABOT Jean*
41. ROUX René
42. SEQUERA Joachim
43. SÉROUGNE Jean*
44. SOUCHAL Roger
45. SOUILLE Gabriel
46. SOUILLE Roland
47. TOURET Jean*
48. TREMBLAY Jacques*
49. VOLLAUD Alfred

(Those names marked with an asterisk are the names of men who did not return.)

However, it was not only those who lived in the village of Lacapelle-Biron who were caught up in the raid. Others who simply happened to be in the area found themselves trapped; others such as **Chopart, Roland** who features on a list of deportees from the villages and towns surrounding Lacapelle. On 21 May 1944, they were all arrested along with the *Capelains*.

Roland *Chopart* is in fact Roland Chopard. The 't' is a misspelling, according to Roland's daughter Annie. Chopart is the name that appears on the two prisoner (*Häftling*) identity cards that Annie found among his papers: *Häftl.-Nr.* 72433 and *Häftl.-Nr.* 75353.

•

Imagine how it would feel to be plucked from your daily life, transported far from home and forced to work in some unknown and terrible place. Imagine being treated with violence, never having enough to eat, living in bestial conditions and never knowing if you would see your home again. Imagine feeling so completely powerless.

We who were born in Europe thought this could never happen to us. We thought that we were safe from being rounded up, taken away, our families left not knowing where we were; we believed ourselves safe from those with authority over us because that's what we were used to.

Except what we are used to no longer exists. Post-Brexit UK and a USA trying to rediscover what its values are following the Trump presidency no longer resemble those architects of the post-Second World War era in Europe. Those certainties, those expectations that we were, at the very least, safer, can now no longer be trusted.

•

One fine day in May 1944, towards the end of the Second World War, while running an errand in rural southwestern France, young Frenchman Roland Chopard was taken by the occupying German army. He was twenty-seven years old, married with a very young son. He was kept in a camp with others, knowing nothing, marched to unknown destinations, put on trains to unknown places, kept in work camps in unfamiliar locations, worked like an animal but not fed as well, and ultimately, made responsible for burying the bodies of those murdered by his captors. And all the while, feeling helpless, angry, brutalised and starving.

Why? How? Could it happen to any one of us, now, today, in Britain, France, Germany, Poland and so on? The posing of that question might have seemed outlandish in 2020 when this introduction was first drafted. Since then, Russia has invaded Ukraine (February 2022). The answer, therefore, is yes.

•

On an overcast heavy day in December 2019, I took the train and bus to the former concentration camp just on the outskirts of Dachau, an ordinary town about 30km from Munich, commonly tagged with the title 'birthplace of the Nazi movement'.

I had already spent some time looking round Munich's NS-Dokumentationszentrum München (Documentation Centre for the History of National Socialism), surprisingly only opened in May 2015, some seventy years after the end of the Second World War. The centre was built on the site of the former headquarters of the National Socialist German Workers' Party (NSDAP) and became known as the Brown House. The Party had bought the Palais Barlow in 1930, rebuilt it extensively and the Party's leadership moved into the building in 1931. Hitler and private secretary Rudolf Hess went to work there, along with others including the Reich Press Office from where misinformation chief, Joseph Goebbels, Reich Minister of Propaganda and Public Enlightenment to give him his full title, could pump out his lethal materials.

It is interesting that the democratic press was scathing about the new HQ, accusing the Nazi Party of delusions of grandeur.[1]

In 1933, the Nazis came to power violently on a wave of nationalist pride and pain, just fifteen years after the end of the First World War.

The Documentation Centre states its aims as wanting to make visitors ask themselves 'Why should this interest me?' and 'Why is this relevant

---

1   https://www.ns-dokuzentrum-muenchen.de/zentrum/ueber-uns/

today?' In his study of the end of the Nazi regime, *Berlin,* historian Antony Beevor provides answers when he writes that there are few things that reveal more about political leaders and their systems than the way in which they are finally defeated. And the manner of their defeat is also important when the young, questioning their lives today, look back at history and find something to admire in a regime such as the Third Reich.[2]

I could ask the same questions about the relevance and interest today of Roland Chopard's experiences almost eighty years ago.

On that cold, overcast day on the train to Dachau, I found one answer.

Dachau was the first concentration camp to be built by the Nazi regime, and served as a model for all the later camps. It was policed by SS men (the *Schutzstaffel,* the paramilitary/political police of the Nazi Party). The camp was set up in 1933 to hold political prisoners and over the twelve years of its existence, over 200,000 persons from all over Europe were held there, and in many subsidiary camps. Those murdered there number 41,500.

Descriptions from the Dachau camp memorial site:

•

THE *SCHUBRAUM* (THE 'SHUNT' ROOM)

When the prisoners arrived at the camp, they were subjected to a brutal and degrading admittance procedure. They were sworn at, threatened and beaten up. Their personal information was recorded, and they were lectured by the protective custody camp leader. They were then brought into this room, the *Schubraum,* where they had to hand over their clothing and everything else that they had brought with them. They left the room naked and were taken to the prisoner baths. No prisoner could know if they would ever leave the concentration camp again.

•

THE *KOMMANDANTUR-ARREST* (THE BUNKER)

This was the camp prison, constructed by the prisoners in 1937/38 when the new camp was being built. The official name was the *Kommandantur-*

---
2   Antony Beevor (2003). *Berlin: The Downfall: 1945*. London: Penguin Books.

Arrest, the headquarters' detention building, but in Dachau it acquired the name *der Bunker*, the Bunker.

The Bunker was a centre of terror. Prisoners were locked in its cells for weeks or months at a time, often in darkness and with even less food than in the rest of the camp. The SS maltreated and tortured prisoners. Additional instruments of torture were installed in 1944, the *Stehzellen*, standing cells. How many prisoners were murdered or driven to suicide in the Bunker is unknown.

From 1941, the *Geheime Staatspolizei* or *Gestapo*, the secret police, also held prominent prisoners in the Bunker as hostages of the regime. In the same year, 1941, a penal camp for members of the police and the SS was set up in the left wing of the building.

After the liberation, the American military administration held Nazi war criminals in custody in the building. Later the building became a military prison for members of the US army.

•

Words from the Dachau site:

'You are without rights, dishonourable and defenceless. You're a pile of shit and that is how you're going to be treated.' (From the address by the protective custody camp leader, Josef Jarolin, to the new prisoners, 1941/42.)

•

'When we arrived in Dachau, dragged from the train to the camp and beaten into a corner there, a kind of public interrogation began from an entire herd of so-called officers… Every nasty joke was received with applause. Every bit of indecency was met with vile laughter.' (From *Time Without Mercy*, an account by Rudolf Kalmar, held in Dachau from 1938–1945.)

•

'I do not know if the reader can imagine what it means when nearly 250 straw mattresses, most of them torn, just as many head rests, and

500 blankets, not to mention the furniture and meagre private belongings, are lying all in a tumble in the dirt and rain; and when these have to be put away, the beds set up, the rooms swept and dusted, the block street cleaned of even the smallest straw, and all during the one-hour break from work.' (From *Priestblock 25487: A Memoir of Dachau*, by Jean Bernard, imprisoned in Dachau in 1941–42.)

•

'Undress, get going, fast! We entered… a large, long hall. Square columns supported the ceiling… Between them stood tables that divided the whole room into two parts. Posters hung above the tables: From A–K, from K–P, etc. Behind these barriers stood a few men with shaved heads, striped suits, and intelligent faces.

'Our personal possessions were once again registered. An SS man in the background shouted "forward, faster."

'The SS man who had brought us ordered: "Undress, get going, faster! Clothing and underwear, everything in one pile!"' (From *As a Prisoner in Dachau*, by Edgar Kupfer-Koberwitz, imprisoned from 1940–1945, describing the admissions procedure in the *Schubraum*.)

•

'… Everything here is pure bluff and devised to torment us. Often they come and rip out the beds, throwing the sheets and blankets all over the place. One of the overlords merely needs to be in a bad mood or have had a bit too much to drink. If he thinks one of the beds is badly made, then he will write up the name of the person, who then receives a report. The punishment for that is one hour pole hanging.' (From *The Powerful and the Helpless*, also by Edgar Kupfer-Koberwitz.)

•

When I was looking round the camp, I came finally to the crematoria. And this was where I found an answer about the relevance of Roland Chopard's story.

German schoolchildren, adolescents about fourteen years old, were running in and out of the shower chamber where many prisoners were sent to be gassed before their bodies were burnt in the ovens. They were giggling and joking, presumably because it's all too long ago, too far-fetched. They are young; this is not their yesterday, but the yesterday of their grandparents.

Nazi has become a useful shorthand for something or someone who disagrees with you. My German-American husband has been called a Nazi on several occasions. It's such a lazy epithet. It is important to recall what 'Nazi' and Nazism really signify.

•

When Roland Chopard set off on his bike from his home in Fumel towards his aunt's house in Monflanquin in the Lot-et-Garonne region of France to get some fresh food supplies, he was well prepared, his knapsack filled with refreshments and paper to wrap up the eggs he was hoping to find. A few kilometres from his destination, he was arrested by the SS Das Reich division, a division still talked about as among the most merciless of the German army, during one of their brutal *rafles* (roundups). Roland's capture seems to have been completely accidental. He cycled into the organised raid being carried out through the region by the SS on the hunt for members of the Resistance, stashes of weapons, people in hiding.

Roland was taken initially to the camp at Compiègne. This was the start of a period of detention and forced labour during which he was moved to different camps, including Dachau, BMW's Eisenach factory and ultimately Buchenwald. He remained in captivity for over a year.

A couple of years after his return home in 1945, Roland felt compelled to write an account of his experiences, producing over 100 pages of clear-sighted, sometimes lyrical, description and analysis. He did not share this with anyone. It remained among his other papers – old identity documents with their official stamps, journals, letters – all stored, unread, in the family house in Villeneuve-sur-Lot. This account forms the basis of the book.

However, Roland Chopard did not exist in isolation, even if he felt as alone as anyone ever has. Years later, his daughter Annie remains haunted by the experiences in his account, revealed to her only after her father's death, and this is partly her story too.

Some years after Roland's death in 2006, Annie's brother Alex was looking through their father's papers and found an exercise book containing the handwritten story of his deportation and life as a slave labourer in Germany.

Both children knew their father had written down his experiences from the day of his capture to his release from Buchenwald, but he had hardly spoken about the war, apart from mentioning one or two incidents. Roland turned these incidents into comic tales, deflecting any more serious interest that his children might have displayed about his wartime experiences. 'And that was that,' says Annie. Alex tried to read the account, 'but found it quite daunting,' says Annie, 'the writing is very small, intricate.' She decided that 'something had to be done now. If not, this story would be lost forever.' Thus began the 'labour of love', which was both rewarding and very frustrating. So many questions that might have been asked but weren't.

Alex also found letters written by Roland to his family, along with other writings, and various documents and artefacts that bring to dramatic life the times he lived through. Annie read through these writings by her beloved father, all done in the immaculate handwriting that French schoolchildren were taught to use, and painstakingly typed them out. Annie asked me to translate his memoir into English and as we discussed the details of the translation, it became clear that it could form the basis of a book. Roland's experiences, shared by so many, are becoming history as those who lived through them and their immediate descendants are dying or dead.

Annie remembers her father as an affectionate and loving man. In his memoir, however, his hatred of his German captors becomes profound as he experiences repeated and pointless acts of barbarity and witnesses scenes of human depravity beyond imagining. When she first read the memoir, Annie was shocked by the intense hatred expressed by the man she had only ever seen as benign and compassionate. One of the most striking things she told me early in our discussions was that it felt as if she had not really known her father. She grew up with someone who had moulded himself into the good father; he never revealed to his children what he had endured. Paradoxically this has made Annie feel guilty. Should she have asked him more questions about his wartime experiences? Should she have been more *interested*? And in some ways, this adult guilt of a grown-up, indeed elderly, child adds to her sense of bereavement and loss.

The memoir contains detailed descriptions of the journeys in train wagons designed for livestock, of the desperate conditions in the work camps, of the physical realities – pain, discomfort, lice everywhere – and the dominating desires for enough food to assuage the constant hunger, and for cigarettes. What stands out particularly from Roland's account is his ability to analyse his situation. He is clear-sighted, pitiless in fact, about how misery and fear affect human behaviour and of the moral degradation attendant upon the brutalisation of human beings. He is as honest about himself as he is about his companions.

•

When Buchenwald was liberated in April 1945 by US forces,[3] Roland was given a rabbit-skin jacket, although he could not remember whether it was given to him by the Red Cross or by the Americans.

At the same time as Alex was rummaging among his father's belongings after Roland's death and found the exercise book with the story of his imprisonment, he also came across this rabbit-skin jacket.

'It was so small, it looked more like a child's jacket,' says Annie. It had always been kept in a trunk in the garage at the family home in Villeneuve-sur-Lot. Annie took the jacket and kept it, also in the garage, in her house in England.

The German jacket, lined with rabbit skin, that was given to Roland during liberation of the prisoners from the Buchenwald camp

....

3   US Holocaust Memorial Museum: https://www.ushmm.org/learn/timeline-of-events/1942-1945/us-forces-liberate-buchenwald

Five years later, in 2011, it was Annie's husband, Nathan, who became curious about the jacket. What would become of it once they died? Would it simply be thrown into a skip – this small piece of history? They decided to contact the Imperial War Museum in London, ultimately donating the jacket and Roland's papers to the museum.

But the jacket was just the start of what was to become Annie's mission to enable her father to speak and to enable her to feel finally that she had asked those questions that should have been asked during his lifetime. Publishing his memoir is a way of keeping Roland's young self alive and of allowing Annie to reassure herself that she has done all she can to honour him and his suffering.

•

Two other memoirs about life as a captive of the Germans during the Second World War have been published in English (that I have found) and I have drawn on these testimonies to give the background to Roland Chopard's own account, as well as drawing on the collections of other contemporary accounts. I have depended on the work of established historians to set Roland's memoir in context, but in magpie fashion, I have dwelt particularly on those sections that aid my understanding and my ability to present Roland's memoir in a way that may add to the reader's understanding. This is intended to be read as a personal story set in a particular time, nothing more but nothing less.

In his memoir, written in 1943, Jean Hélion describes the experiences of this artist turned soldier who was captured in woodlands near the small village of Billy, located in the Loir-et-Cher department in the Centre region, after the rout of the French army in the spring and summer of 1940.[4] He ended up in Germany as a prisoner of war working for the conquering enemy. Hélion and a fellow POW carried out a daring escape in 1942, and he made it to the USA. There he flourished as an artist.

The book is a series of scenes, detailed and vivid, with a certain breathless quality almost as if written while the events were taking place. Hélion

---

4   Jean Hélion (2014). *They Shall Not Have Me: The Capture, Forced Labor, and Escape of a French Prisoner in World War II*. New York: Skyhorse Publishing Inc.

wrote it after his escape directly in English – no need for a translator – in response to a request from the US Office of War Information in aid of the Allied war effort. The war was still far from being over when he started writing the memoir – the brutal Battle of Stalingrad was still continuing. It wasn't clear how the war would end.

The second, quite different, memoir is by Elie Poulard, who as a very young man of twenty-two was forced into hard labour in Germany under the requirements of the notorious Vichy government legislation, known as the Service du Travail Obligatoire (STO). Unlike Hélion, Poulard did not write down his memories of that time immediately after his return home. He was able to tell anecdotes and stories about what he experienced, often encouraged by his brother Jean V. Poulard's questions, but it was not until 1994 that Jean Poulard prevailed upon his brother to write them down. He was then able to translate the manuscript into English and set it in context.[5]

The experiences of these 'French slaves', as Poulard called them, have not been in the spotlight as much as other events of that war. More than 650,000 French men (mainly men, as Vichy feared the reactions of the people and the Church if women were also called up) are known to have been conscripted into the STO, without counting those like Roland Chopard, caught up in the frenzy of the final year of the war in Europe. This may be for a variety of reasons, not least the unwillingness of people to examine those things in our past that hurt, shame and disturb us so much. In his introduction to his brother's memoir, Jean Poulard notes that after their liberation, those young men who had been forced to work for the Germans under the STO law were often treated upon their return to France as if they had been collaborators. They were treated with suspicion rather than sympathy.

Most movingly, I have also drawn on another very personal resource, the spoken testimonies of the relatives of those men who were deported during the raid on Lacapelle-Biron in which Roland was trapped. The Association de Mémoire Vive[6] produced a film of these witnesses in which they talk directly about their memories of that day in May 1944 when

---

5   Elie Poulard (2016.) Translated and edited by Jean V Poulard. *A French Slave in Nazi Germany: A Testimony.* Notre Dame, Indiana: University of Notre Dame Press.
6   *La Rafle au Coeur, Lacapelle-Biron 21 May 1944.* A film by Bernard Semerjian, Jacques Augié and Myriam Semerjian.

some of them saw their fathers for the last time. They talk as if the events had happened just hours ago.

However, in the early part of the twenty-first century, we are now seeing a full forgetting of our shared European past and a desire to distort and make use of the parts that most serve our various causes. Brexit is an example of this cynical manipulation of a deliberately simplified history in pursuit of an invented ideal, which in any case is a cover for financial gain, political gain and personal short-term ambition. Beware those who sell you an easy version of history.

The personal experience of Roland Chopard, which he describes with such vividness and feeling, should remind us how dangerous it is to let the past be commandeered by those who are ignorant enough to think truth doesn't matter.

ONE

'OÙ EST ROL?'

'Où est Rol? Où est Rol?'

This is what Annie remembers as a little girl, her mother calling out repeatedly, 'Where is Rol? Where is Rol?'

Her parents would joke about it, this constant need of Irène to know Roland's whereabouts – her small, prim and proper mum, and her bubbly, funny father. It is only later, much later, both parents dead and Annie a mature woman, that she understands. For almost a year, Irène had no idea where he was, what had happened to him, whether he was even alive. All she knew was that he had been taken by German soldiers while out on an errand and that she had been abandoned to fend for herself and for Alex, their one-year-old son.

Roland before his deportation

The last Irène saw of Roland before he was transported from the holding camp in Agen to the internment camp at Compiègne was on the tenth day of his imprisonment, the beautiful last day of May 1944. Roland writes:

'On that day, in fact at around 14:00 hours, we were given the order to pack our bags. It was a simple enough task to gather up our rags, carefully clutch a few rare relics, bundle up the last supplies.'

The prisoners were moved in columns, three at a time, across the grounds, then through the wide-open 'great iron gate'.

'Outside, some of us saw our loved ones for a last time. My wife and my mother were there. I was the last one in the column so they thought for a moment, for a brief instant, that I wasn't part of this bleak convoy. But all of a sudden, they caught sight of me. Their grief weighed on me more than my own sorrow.'

His mother and Irène followed the prisoners to the train station where the cattle cars waited.

'Then the sliding doors, creaking and grinding, closed on their cargo and shut us in the shadows. A last blown kiss, then darkness.'

•

Roland and Irène might have hoped that by May 1944 they had survived the worst of the war and the Occupation, that there might be some hope for the future, that their lives might be lived peacefully. Roland was a very young man, a civilian who had survived much already in his twenty-seven years, including the typically self-sufficient existence of a colonial childhood split between France and West Africa, and military service:

'I was twenty years old and what was I to do? I had to complete military service: do it now or ask for a deferment so I could get on with my studies. Given the digressions, the folly, the incoherence of my past academic life, I chose to do my military service. And so I knowingly let myself into two years of complete physical and mental deprivation. I lost two years of my youth without any compensation. Sport had been my motivation but I couldn't do it anymore. And then came the war and complete degeneration…'

By 1944, Roland was working as a clerical officer at the local steel factory in Fumel in the Lot-et-Garonne department in southwestern France. He met and fell in love with local girl Irène David and they married on 6 March 1943.

Born on 27 January 1922, Irène was five years younger than Roland, small, rather stylish, well groomed with a wide-eyed smile despite her shyness. She was an intensely religious young woman. Annie is close to tears when she reads aloud to me some of Irène's writings from old exercise books that Annie has kept. Both Irène and Roland evidently loved to write, making notes, considering their lives, recording their thoughts, and, in Irène's case, prayers and verses.

Upon their engagement, Roland writes:

'Irène, tu revêts les qualités inhérentes à la véritable jeune fille. Tu es celle que j'avais toujours rêvée, pure comme un crépuscule d'été, désirable comme une fleur fraîchement éclose, jolie comme une miniature.' (Irène, you have all the attributes a young woman should have. You are the one I always dreamed of, pure as summer twilight, desirable as a newly unfurled flower, pretty as a figurine.)

They complemented each other in every way. Roland writes of how her refreshing way of thinking *(fraîcheur de pensée)* acts as a balm for his perhaps over-serious approach *(la maturité précoce de mon esprit)*. Did this maturity, unusual in such a young man and typical of someone used to fending for themselves, help Roland to hang on to his sanity during the imprisonment that lay ahead of him?

Irène was the daughter of Elise Amouroux and Pierre David, who had particular ideas about how to treat a child.

'He was strict, very strict, very very strict,' Annie tells me. 'Just a look was enough. Mum used to tell me a story. They were eating chicken, and Mum pointed at the thigh and said *"Je veux ça"* (I want that) and he told her not to point and sent her to her room without having anything to eat.'

Like many women of her generation, Irène was barred from fulfilling ambitions to continue her studies and instead learnt shorthand and worked as a secretary at the same factory in Fumel where her husband worked. 'She was very intelligent, took the school certificate at fourteen. She would have liked to continue with her studies, go to university, but it wasn't possible financially,' says Annie.

(And later, when she and Roland moved to Sénégal, in what was then the colonial territory known as Afrique-Occidentale Française, French West Africa, after the war, she continued to study, taking exams, and ultimately becoming a *secrétaire de direction* [executive secretary]. Nevertheless, in her heart she would have loved to study more. 'She was always an avid reader,' says Annie.)

By 1944, the young couple were both juggling full-time jobs at the steel factory with looking after their baby son Alex. Irène's mother-in-law, Rose Euphreusine Boneil, stepped in to help, or at least, that was the idea. In truth, Rose's help was quite specific and did not, Irène discovered, involve housework.

Annie remembers how her mother used to talk about Rose. (This was always going to be a fraught relationship.) When Irène arrived home from a full day's work at the factory, she was welcomed with both baby son Alex and a pile of dirty terry cloth nappies stiff with their dried contents. Irène would mutter to herself, 'Why didn't she even think to soak the nappies?' But all she could do was sigh and say to herself, *'Ah bon, voilà.'* (So that's how it is).

And years later, Irène would tell daughter Annie about those Sundays in the early days of Alex's babyhood. Rose used to take Alex out, showing him off – he was so *'mignon'* (cute). But Irène didn't put her feet up. Irène had to continue to do the housework. *'Alors de ce côté-là, elle n'a pas eu beaucoup d'aide'* (she didn't get a lot of help on that front).

Roland's life, barely begun, was defined by work and family. His and Irène's concerns were intensely domestic. They had to get by, like everyone else, in spite of the war, in spite of the Occupation. But theirs was a deeply loving relationship, which must have allayed some of the everyday underlying anxiety. Day to day life continued.

•

By May 1944 when Roland's life was about to be interrupted in the most terrifying way, it had been four long years since the summer of 1940 and the shockingly rapid defeat of the French army over six desperate weeks through May–June of that year. The chaos and trauma that followed led to years of confusion and doubt. French citizens were driven to try to accommodate the invaders to a greater or lesser extent, or to resist them. The story of how French people reacted to their trauma continues to be examined and retold. For many, it was simply a question of how to survive.

It must be remembered that the First World War had ended only twenty-two years before. Memories were still fresh for many. People were exhausted, still scarred. Society was fragmenting.

Roland's own uncle, Gaston, who was his grandparents' second son of four, was called up to fight in the First World War with huge consequences for himself and his family, especially his mother. The post-war life that Gaston led is described by Roland without comment, in a way that is pared down, simple and devastating.

'The second son Gaston led an unusual life and remained a confirmed bachelor. He was called up to fight in the 14–18 war. I know nothing of the campaigns he was involved in except that he was a victim of poison gas. Because of this, he received a war pension. After this episode, he went back to his village and lived with his mother. He became a true woodsman, living a solitary, taciturn, independent life. As a poacher of both game and fish, he was the target of the police and gamekeepers but was never caught.

'Cunning and swift, always wearing his wooden clogs lined with straw, he made his way around the countryside, through the forest, past the rivers and streams. The cops shouted after him in vain as they pursued him. Apart from this illegal activity that was so much a part of his nature, he busied himself in quieter moments making the clogs which were what most people wore in the countryside at that time. Work that he carried out very skilfully.

'But sometimes, his disability provoked in him angry outbursts that were more spectacular than effective. This inspired some fear in those surrounding him (brother, nephews and nieces who met up on occasion). When these episodes happened, everyone dodged out of the way and left him alone in the company of his mother who was the only one who was able to calm him down. As he grew older, he became more balanced, more sensible and ended his days in the same house where he had always lived.'

However, Gaston's post-war life was not entirely lived in the natural world where he had more control over the killing and was himself hunter, not hunted. His experience as a woodsman led him to participate in the Resistance during the next war. During the years of Occupation, this man 'who was rebellious by nature' took part in the Resistance and may even have been deported, according to Roland. And Chopard family lore has it that he may even have been friends with *Chanoine* (Canon) Kir, a priest and keenly political man who helped many prisoners escape from the Longvic camp near Dijon during the Second World War and was resolutely opposed to the German occupiers in Dijon.

And if that name seems familiar, it is because his name has been given to a delicious French aperitif known as Kir, white wine (*bourgogne aligoté* for the purists) with a dash of *crème de Cassis* (blackcurrant syrup). The Canon used to serve this drink at official ceremonies in Dijon where he was Deputy Mayor.

•

The First World War had ended in 1918. Only twenty-two years later, it was all happening again. On 14 June 1940, Paris fell to the invading German army. All efforts to appease Hitler had not worked. The French Prime Minister Paul Raynaud had rejected the policy of appeasement, but this was not a majority view. The French government had abandoned Paris, initially moving to Tours, then on to Bordeaux, fleeing the German army. On 16 June, Reynaud resigned and was succeeded by the traditional and ultra-conservative deputy Prime Minister Marshal Philippe Pétain, a hero of the first war, who preferred an armistice with Germany. This was a development welcomed by French people, by and large, so tired and frightened were they, so in need of reassurance.

The reasons for France's collapse are many and well-examined.[7] For its citizens, the effects were profound. France became, literally, a divided country, with resistance and collaboration co-existing in a broken society.

The French government finally ended up in the spa town of Vichy in the Auvergne-Rhône-Alpes region of central France, after the signing on 25 June of the Armistice agreement imposed by Germany. On 9–10 July, parliament met up in this town to discuss the future of France. Underlying their discussions of how to shape that future was the acceptance that the war was over, and that Germany had won. (Paxton, p. 11.) Of course, the war was not over, but for Vichy the aim was to restore some kind of normalcy, to allow its citizens to return home, to encourage everyday life to continue. Vice premier Pierre Laval was instrumental in persuading the parliament to vote for the end of the Third Republic, paving the way for a government of

---

7   Robert O. Paxton (1972. New introduction 2001). *Vichy France: Old Guard and New Order 1940–1944*. Originally published: New York: Knopf, 1972. Columbia University Press, 2001.

'national unity' that would seek collaboration with the German occupiers. The word collaboration, meaning simply working together, came to symbolise the worst of human behaviour, the willingness to be complicit in evil.

France was essentially cut in two: the northern Occupied Zone, occupied by the Germany army and the southern unoccupied zone, administered by the Vichy regime, called the *'zone libre'* (Free Zone). The situation was not as clear-cut as that, however. Vichy's civil jurisdiction extended throughout the whole of metropolitan France, excluding the disputed territory of Alsace-Lorraine, placed under German administration.

Vichy sought to restore internal order and to address such pressing concerns as Occupation costs, operation of the demarcation line between the zones, the liberation of French prisoners of war, and the return of the government to Paris. (Paxton, p. 76). The government never intended to stay in Vichy – but it never escaped.

•

Young Frenchman Elie Poulard, living through those tense, unforgiving and fearful months of the *Drôle de guerre*, the phony war, before the invasion, tells the story of how a retired Norwegian consul living in his village of Mareuil with his wife and skinny daughter (so skinny that other girls called her *une aiguille fine* – 'a fine needle') was killed by members of the French home guard. They alleged the consul had given signals to German planes, resulting in an attack on the village on 10 May.

Poulard's memoir of his time as a forced labourer, translated by brother Jean, is one of the very few such memoirs published in English (see Introduction). He grew up in Mareuil-sur-Ay in the Marne valley, location of two terrible battles during the First Word War. No child in France could avoid the symbols of that war, continually evoked through the military cemeteries, the monuments to the fallen. Elie, like many others, was obsessed by the fear that he too might be caught up in another war, another blaze of horror.

Back to the night of 10 May 1940, and the attack on the village, Elie was recovering from illness at home in bed. Around midnight, he got up to be sick. He and his father heard the noise of engines and machine guns coming from aeroplanes. It was the end of the phony war, the beginning of the real one.

Soon the village was overflowing with people coming from the Ardennes in Belgium and troop convoys going in the opposite direction towards Belgium. The house next door to Elie's was used to store explosives. He writes that there was always a truck in front of their house which was full to the hilt with enough explosives to blow up most of the village. (Poulard, p. 8.)

That spring and summer was a time of terrible confusion and fear. Jean Hélion was a well-known French artist by the outbreak of the war and a volunteer in the French army. He was taken prisoner by the Germans, but managed to escape two years later, fleeing to the USA. In 1943, he wrote his memoir in English (see Introduction). It presents a series of vivid stories about life as a prisoner of war.

Roland Chopard was still living the life of a happily married civilian while Hélion was recovering from his imprisonment in the USA.

Roland's ordeal was yet to come.

On 14 June 1940, Hélion was watching the motley column moving out of a village west of Paris – loaded farm vehicles being pulled by horses, people on foot, cattle, cars pulling trailers – and he had a sudden flash of recognition. Twenty-two years earlier, he and his mother were also forced to flee from the north. Jean's mother was pushing the cart with all their belongings. He remembered that her feet were bleeding. All around them the skies were lit up in the reds and blues of flares and explosions as the Battle of the Somme raged. At sunrise, the boy Jean looked around him. He noticed a woman ahead of them wearing simply her dressing gown and carrying an alarm clock, while beside her there was a girl pulling a wheelbarrow containing her mother. The woman, her jaw slack, was covered in various bundles that were falling off onto the road. It was clear the woman was dead, but the girl was unaware. (Hélion, p. 15.)

In June 1940 the thirty-six-year-old Hélion finds himself once again caught in the chaos of war as the defeated French army regroups here and there among those fleeing the fallen capital. He wonders where the so-called famed French army is now, where all the generals have gone. And he is hungry. He and his fellow soldiers come across a pile of eggs in an abandoned chicken house and swallow them raw. (Hélion, p. 27.)

In those days, hours and months following the rout of the French army, people were confused, frightened, apprehensive about the future and uncertain who to trust. How could anyone know what to do next? Society was already fractured in any case. People were bitterly divided, politicians continued feuding, the economy had turned sour under the effects of the Great Depression, the threat of right-wing violence was growing, there was intense xenophobia leading to a protectionist attitude opposed to foreign goods and foreign workers, and with the collapse in 1937 of the left-wing Popular Front led by socialist prime minister Léon Blum, France had gone seriously off the rails. The Third Republic was in crisis.

After the fall of the Blum government, experienced centre-left politician Edouard Daladier, who was Blum's Minister of National Defence, took over as head of government. And on 30 September 1938, it was Edouard Daladier, like Marshal Pétain, also a distinguished veteran of the First World War, who signed the Munich Pact with Hitler, along with his counterparts in Italy, Benito Mussolini, and in Britain, Neville Chamberlain, thereby delivering Czechoslovakia to the German state in the name of peace. On 15 March 1939, Germany invaded Czechoslovakia. On 3 September, Britain and France had declared war on Germany. And by the following summer, Paris had fallen.

The different narratives of who France was, what it stood for during the terrible years of the Second World War, may each represent one aspect of the truth, but any one single narrative does not represent the whole truth. Complexity and ambiguity, full-on hypocrisy, fear and fatigue, corruption and courage, all jostled in the awful soup of occupation. Even the famed French Resistance, ultimate popular symbol of the admirable sort of patriotism and the upholder of all that is good in humanity, was a mash-up of different factions with different ideologies.

France was an occupied country.

For French people, life became an accommodation with their own powerlessness. How did they survive?

Food (the lack of), fear (always present) and the longing for 'normality' (what did that mean anymore?) were their constant preoccupations.

•

THE CHANTIERS DE JEUNESSE

In the summer and autumn of 1940, a pressing problem had to be dealt with. What was to be done about all the young men who were left with nothing to do once France had been invaded and the agreement with the German occupiers was signed?

It was still uncertain whether the war was over with the fall of France. Propaganda sheets circulating in the holding camp where Jean Hélion fetched up after his capture blamed France for the war, the British for secretly driving them to it. Hitler was misunderstood, forced into a war he did not want by 'international plutocrats' (code for Jews). He would carry through his mission – the unification of Europe under German command for everlasting peace. (Hélion, p. 93.)

It had been agreed under the Armistice terms that compulsory military service would be suspended and this, coupled with the dissolution of the French army which would now have to demobilise its young conscripts, meant that there had to be a plan. In 1940, Marshal Pétain was developing the notion of a paramilitary force crossed with scout camp as a means of keeping the young males occupied. General Joseph de la Porte du Theil was charged with dealing with all these twenty-year-old young men, some 100,000 of them called up on 9 and 10 June, now wandering the streets not so much looking for weapons as looking for something to eat.[8] (Amouroux, p. 347.)

Thus, the Chantiers de la Jeunesse came into being on 30 July 1940 and a couple of days later, the first young recruits were attached to their unit of the Chantiers for a period of six months. The programme continued to evolve. In January 1941, the time period was extended to eight months, replacing military service, and in March 1943, the Chantiers was placed directly under the authority of the head of government.[9] The idea was to offer a physical and moral education to these young men – a communal working life lived in camps, away from civilian society, lives full of fresh air and manly vigour, what Amouroux calls a *'pétainisme viril'* (virile Pétainism). (Amouroux, p. 353.) They were run essentially according to the credo of the Marshal, and their teachers and mentors were young and former soldiers. In fact, these young men proved to be a fertile recruiting ground for the Resistance – probably not what the Marshal had in mind.

....

8   Henri Amouroux (1961, 1990, 2011 paperback edition). *La Vie des Français sous l'Occupation*. Paris: Librairie Arthème Fayard.
9   https://francearchives.fr/findingaid/56e74bc24e7da43a36a215df123c2f3256b11d0c

General de la Porte du Theil's aim was to instil in these young men a sense of patriotism and solidarity with the goal of creating an army, a substitute for the compulsory military service banished by the Germans. Young French Jews were excluded, first in North Africa, then in mainland France. In July 1942 the general proposed a law excluding Jews from the Chantiers to the Commissariat Général aux Questions Juives (General Commission on Jewish Affairs). This was quickly approved by the Commission, established by the Vichy government, keen to fall in with its German occupiers.

And in fact, shortly after this law was proposed, in a joint operation between the German and French administrations, Jews were rounded up and confined in the Vélodrome d'Hiver (an indoor cycle track) in Paris, before being sent to their deaths in the extermination camps. The journey itself in sealed cattle wagons caused many to die from lack of food and water.

The events at the Vel d'Hiv, as it is known, have become bitterly symbolic of French collaboration with the occupiers. Some 4,500 French policemen began arresting foreign Jews living in Paris on 16 July 1942. They arrested more than 11,000 Jews on that same day, and within the week, the number of Jews held had risen to 13,000. Among them were 4,000 children. Conditions in the Vel d'Hiv were disgusting – crowded, unsanitary, little food or water. The detainees were moved on to the concentration camps in Pithiviers and Beaune-la-Rolande in the Loiret region south of Paris, and to Drancy, near Paris. Parents and families were then separated from their children and deported, most of them to Auschwitz. The forcibly abandoned children were left alone in these French camps before being deported to Auschwitz in the company of adults they didn't know in the sealed railway wagons.[10]

•

Most of Vichy's remaining autonomy and authority was destroyed in November 1942, in direct consequence of the Anglo-American landings in North Africa. On November 11, 1942, German troops were ordered by Hitler to cross the demarcation line that had cut France in two in 1940, and to enter the unoccupied zone to take over the whole country. The Vichy government survived, but without the power and authority it wielded previously. It only

---

10 https://www.yadvashem.org/holocaust/france/vel-dhiv-roundup.html

lingered on because Germany allowed it to. Vichy nevertheless waged war in collaboration with the Germans against French citizens, pursuing the Resistance cells that were gathering force, cooperating enthusiastically in hunting them out with the aid of the paramilitaries, the French *milices*.

When the Germans invaded the *Zone Libre* and dissolved the Armistice army, they didn't disband the Chantiers de Jeunesse, although they were reorganised. The Germans suspected them of providing a good fomenting ground for resistance. Even so, the young were being looked after, so why disturb what would also be a good source of manpower for the German state with their own young dispatched to war? The Chantiers thus became a sort of trap for thousands of young Frenchmen compelled to work in Germany. There is a clear line to be drawn between the Chantiers and the establishment in February 1943 of the Service du Travail Obligatoire (STO), the forced labour organisation put in place by Vichy under the stewardship of Prime Minister Pierre Laval.

Laval had previously championed the use of another programme, known as la Relève, precursor to the fully fledged STO. This was supposed to be a prisoner repatriation scheme, exchanging a French prisoner of war for three skilled French workers deployed to work in German factories. Germany was agitating for much more effort from Vichy to supply workers to its factories as by 1942 it had pretty much exhausted the supply of Polish and Russian labourers, many of them worked to death. (Paxton, p. 310.) The order was given in May 1942 by Fritz Sauckel,[11] described as Hitler's chief recruiter of slave labour, to authorise the use of force to obtain labour from all occupied countries. Laval offered the Relève as a way out of this problem, but this ploy could not meet the quota demanded by Sauckel and by February 1943, Vichy instituted the conscription of whole age groups.

When Elie Poulard talks about la Relève, he is scathing, arguing that it was both fraudulent and a failure. People who had been in the habit of looking up to Marshal Pétain were now questioning their devotion and even burning portraits of the old man that they had been keeping in their homes. (Poulard, p. 19.)

The Chantiers were finally disbanded 10 June 1944, a scant twenty days since Roland Chopard had been rounded up and dispatched in a

....
11 https://www.britannica.com/biography/Fritz-Sauckel

train meant for livestock to work in Germany. It is estimated that around 300,000–500,000 young men passed through the Chantiers and of this number, some 16,000 were sent directly to work under the auspices of the STO. (French Archives.)

Vichy offered the rule of traditional authoritarian Marshal Pétain, who was not shy about collaborating with the occupiers, but in fact zealous in his willingness to do their bidding. The Vichy government he led claimed to be acting as a shield against the German demand for forced labour and the export of Jews. This is disputed. Paxton notes that this was not at all as effective as those defending Vichy claimed. (Paxton, p. 365.)

Pétain had offered *'le don de ma personne'* (the gift of my person) to the French people in his radio address of 17 June 1940. They accepted it gladly. By 1944, when Roland was taken, Pétain had become an enemy.

•

THE SERVICE DU TRAVAIL OBLIGATOIRE (STO)

French men and women had been encouraged to volunteer to work in Germany from the early days of the Occupation; Germany was appealing essentially to those looking for work. The regime sought workers from the occupied nations to replace its own young. It was desperate for manpower to feed its factories, particularly once its soldiers were engaged in fighting the Soviet Union on the Eastern Front from the spring of 1942.

'L'Allemagne vous offre du travail' (Germany offers you work) proclaimed the posters. Such posters were powerful tools of competing propaganda, to the extent that the occupying Germans ensured the necessary supplies of materials to produce them even though there were shortages everywhere.[12] The number of French men and women who took up this offer as volunteers are estimated at somewhere around 40,000–72,000. (Amouroux, p. 359.)

However, as the German need for labour continued to swell and its demands on the Vichy administration became ever more intense, and with the failure of Laval's Relève scheme, the Vichy government was forced to

....
12 Margaret Collins Weitz (01 Jan 2000). *Art in the Service of Propaganda: The Poster War in France during World War II*. Religion and the Arts, Volume 4: Issue 1, pp. 43–75. Publisher: Brill. https://doi.org/10.1163/15685290152126412

pass a law in September 1942 requiring the conscription of all able-bodied men aged eighteen to fifty and single women aged twenty-one to thirty-five to do any work the government ordered them to do. This law, *'loi du 4 septembre 1942 relative à l'utilisation et à l'orientation de la main-d'œuvre'* (Law of 4 September 1942 on the use and guidance of the workforce), was signed by Pétain as well as by Laval.

In October, Vichy undertook a census of French men and women in these age groups. Provisions were made for men who had served as soldiers, former prisoners of war were not included, nor were fathers of three or more children. Higher rates of pay in Germany were offered as an enticement; the Vichy government, with little power left, supervised the consolidation of French enterprises thereby freeing up workers. The efforts to persuade were intense. Fake news is not a new phenomenon – newspapers published enthusiastic statements and letters from French workers in Germany, lauding the camaraderie, the food, the availability of tobacco. Reporters were recruited to paint a glowing picture of working life in Germany. One example of this effort is the 'best Christmas letter' competition organised by L'Association nationale des amis des travailleurs français en Allemagne (The National Association of the friends of French workers in Germany). The Association received more than 100,000 letters from children in response to its competition. (Amouroux, p. 363.)

Elie Poulard recalls the period following the enactment of the 4 September law as being a dramatic time. He writes that everyone who was forced into working in Germany for the occupiers was already well aware of what was waiting for them – the never-ending hunger which they were already used to, being badly treated and, of course, the bombings. (Poulard, p. 20.)

It seemed you had to obey the law – there was no real place to hide, and in any case, there was always the fear you would be denounced. Some people argued it was good for the young to be sent off to Germany, it would sort them out – an argument that seems to be heard repeatedly at different times and in different eras. As Poulard remarks quite caustically, he was not going to be able to count on them to help him escape. At that time, the Resistance was not really set up to aid escapees in Poulard's region of Champagne-Ardenne in the northwest of France. That would take until the end of the following year.

There were all kinds of reasons not to try to avoid the STO's orders – the principal one being the fear of reprisals against your family. Poulard initially did not respond to the summons to go to the Soissons worksite of the Organisation Todt (Todt Organisation) in France. When the second requisition order arrived, he decided it was impossible not to obey. And at least he wasn't going to Germany... not yet.

The Todt Organisation had a huge reach. A civil and military engineering organisation, it was founded by Fritz Todt, an engineer and keen supporter of Hitler. It grew from Todt's experience of constructing the *Autobahn* (highway) network from 1933 until 1938, drawing on conscripted labour from within Germany. Following the invasion of Poland in 1939, Todt became Minister for Armaments and Munitions and the organisation carried out almost exclusively military projects. This created a huge demand for labourers, for men and boys, leading the organisation to draw from sources well beyond Germany's borders. It became notorious for its use of slave labour. By 1944, the total number of labourers in the service of the organisation, either conscripted or abducted, was about 1.5 million. Many died because of violent mistreatment, poor food, poor lodging and a lack of medical care. Those not needed by the organisation were supplied to other German companies and companies in occupied countries, especially France, which had been given military contracts.[13]

One young inshore fisherman who worked with his father in Barfleur in the Normandy region of Le Cotentin talks about being approached by a young *'collabo'* (collaborator) who tried to recruit him into the Todt company.[14] The fisherman, Louis Pesnel, was in fact conscripted by the Maritime Registration Office and told to report to the German employment agency in Cherbourg in March 1943, one of the ways in which passive collaboration worked. Pesnel says that in his part of the Cotentin, not a single fisherman tried to escape conscription into the STO. They were among the first to be sent to Germany and there was tacit recognition of this among French officialdom. They were not offered any way out of the situation and at that point, there wasn't much noise coming from the Resistance.

....
13 http://www.Histclo.com/essay/war/ww2/cou/ger/mil/for-todt.html and http://www.wilearncap.asuscomm.com:81/wikipedia_en_all_novid_2017-08/A/Todt_Organization.html
14 http://www.Memoires-de-guerre.fr/?q=en/archive/service-du-travail-obligatoire-compulsory-work-service-parenthesis-several-months/3931

Pesnel lasted some nine months as an STO conscript, but when he returned home on leave – which was starting to look as if it might be forbidden because of German fears the French would abscond – Pesnel did indeed decide not to return and hid out in the countryside with his parents' aid, becoming *'un clandestin'*. (He was not alone – of the 758 conscripts from the department of Manche who came back on leave, some two-thirds did not return.)

•

The term 'forced labour' was not often used at the time, even though it took place on a massive scale during the Second World War. Germans referred to these members of their conscripted workforce as *Fremdarbeiter* (foreign labourers), while the Allies used the term 'slave labour', most notably at the Nuremberg International Military Tribunal in 1945/46.[15] Forced labour for Nazi Germany meant there was no labour contract, or even if there was a contract, the worker did not have the power to terminate it. Forced labourers were essentially powerless, they could be discriminated against and could alter neither their working conditions nor their living conditions. The deportees fell into different categories – deported civilians like Elie Poulard, prisoner of war labourers like Jean Hélion, those deported for political or racist reasons, like Roland Chopard. The stamp on his *Carte de Rapatrié* (identity card for returnees) is authorised by the Ministère des Prisonniers De Guerre, Déportés et Réfugiés.

What made it so particular in France, and so particularly bitter, was the very difficult position those deportees, who had been recruited forcibly under the STO, found themselves in. They had been officially conscripted to serve the German war effort by their own government. A lot of deportees in this category preferred to go into hiding *(réfractaires)* or to join the Resistance *(le maquis)*.

(The Italian-derived term 'maquis' arrived from Corsica and has an interesting history, moving from its use as a common description of woods

---

15 Christoph Thonfeld (2011). *Memories of Former World War Two Forced Labourers – an International Comparison*. Oral History 39, no.2(2011):33-48. http://www.jstor.org/stable/41332163

and scrubland on the island to encompass both rural location and band of fighters. *'Prendre le maquis'*, *'le maquis'* and *'le maquisard'* all became synonymous with the Resistance. Nobody used the term 'maquis' before January 1943, but it was ubiquitous by June.[16])

With the introduction of the Service du Travail Obligatoire in 1943, France was becoming, after Poland, the greatest source of foreign workers for the German war machine. French workers also constituted the largest source of skilled labour in the whole of occupied Europe. (Paxton, p. 311.)

From February 1943, all young men over twenty years old were compelled to go to work in Germany. Recruitment was carried out by whole age groups, that is to say those born between 1920 and 1922. The class of 1942 was the most affected. The promise that farmers or students would be exempted was an empty one. Young women were also supposed to be conscripted under the STO, but in the event, this generally didn't happen because of fears about the reaction of many French people and of the Church.

New demands for another vast contingent of France's young that were issued in April 1943 largely went unfulfilled. They went into hiding, becoming *'clandestins'* like Louis Pesnel or they joined the Resistance. By November 1943, there were more French men working in German factories – over 1.3 million – than there were Russian and Polish men. And the number of French women working for the Germans totalled some 44,000. (Paxton, p. 366.)

•

'OÙ EST ROL?'

Roland was born in 1917 and so had not been requisitioned for work under the STO laws. He was working in the local factory, caring for his family and trying to survive in his rural community in southwestern France.

This was one of the heartlands of the maquis – where resistance flourished.

---

16 H.R. Kedward (1993). *In Search of the Maquis: Rural Resistance in Southern France 1942–1944.* Oxford: Clarendon Press

TWO

ROLAND, *DAS REICH*, RESISTANCE

MAY 1944

By the time the spring of 1944 was coming into full bloom, the situation was much changed in the southwestern region where Roland and Irène were living with their little son Alex, their *'Titou'*. The so-called Free Zone had been under direct German rule for a year and a half. Vichy had little power. The Allied landings were about to happen, but nobody knew this. Daily life seemed set in miserable stone.

Life in the rural south was superficially 'normal'. People worked, married, had families in the usual way, always facing the practical questions of finding sufficient food to put on the table, navigating the bureaucracy under occupation.

The Germans themselves were more commonly seen in the bigger towns and cities, sweeping through in their army vehicles. When they were present in the countryside, it was to seek out those who resisted, those who were hiding out, to spread utter terror.

•

Resistance had started out with student protests, clandestine newspapers, early attempts at intelligence-gathering networks. Ideologically, there was little unity. (Paxton p. 40.) Marshal Pétain's government did not face an organised opposition in those early post-Armistice days, weeks, months and years.

From small and disparate beginnings, however, it had grown into a powerful collection of fighters, and by 1944, had become more focused and formidable, following Germany's move to occupy the whole country, diminish the remaining influence of Vichy and force French citizens into virtual slave labour. *Résistants* might be far apart politically and be aiming for different post-war goals in the future, but they were united in an unflinching determination to fight the Germans, to rid France of its occupiers and to avenge their degradation. In the spring of 1944, the Germans were expecting an Allied invasion and were becoming increasingly brutal in their attempts to repress resistance.

Women, unable to vote in France until 1945, played a hugely significant role. Under Pétain's Vichy government, women's duties were consigned to home and family. Women found themselves resisting not only the occupying Germans, but also all those gender stereotypes. Many fought to prevent their husbands and sons and brothers from being forced to leave France to work in Germany under the STO. Women found themselves abandoning tradition and taking on the work and responsibilities usually assigned to men. And as the Resistance movement grew, the restraints of those traditional roles loosened, and new freedoms opened up. Women were able to engage in different activities where their skills could be put to good use – in intelligence, in propaganda work, in sabotage and sometimes in taking up arms.[17] (Gildea, p. 141.)

The Resistance forces themselves were still widely disparate, with views and ambitions covering the breadth of the political spectrum. The Free French, headed by General de Gaulle, worked closely with the Allies and were waiting for D-Day, while those in the internal Resistance, especially communists, were impatient and wanted action immediately, of whatever kind, in preparation for a wider public uprising after the landings. (Gildea, pp. 314–341.)

In the southwestern area of France where Roland and his family lived, resistance was both widespread and widely supported by the local

....

17 Robert Gildea (2015). *Fighters in the Shadows: A New History of the French Resistance.* London: Faber & Faber Ltd.

inhabitants. The department of the Lot-et-Garonne was right in the heart of Resistance country. Even if Roland and Irène did not take an active part in resistance, they would have been aware of the activities. Roland, certainly, was in complete sympathy with their aims and it is likely that both he and Irène were in agreement, given their deeply compatible relationship. What they didn't share was religious faith. Irène was a deeply religious woman living in Vichy France, led by Marshal Pétain, who after all was the embodiment of a Catholic, authoritarian, paternalist society, its motto being *'Travail, famille, patrie'* – Work, family, country – rather than the republican motto of *'Liberté, égalité, fraternité'* – Freedom, equality, brotherhood. Irène, like many women, was not a stay-at-home mother, but a working woman struggling to stay afloat.

Roland makes several references to the maquis in his memoir. Just after he had been captured and the men were still waiting to find out what was going to happen to them, he talks about the following incident:

'In an insignificant country village, a farmer had been denounced as being in possession of weapons. The Krauts seized him and used multiple threats to try to get him to admit links with the local Resistance. Faced with his denials, they turned his house upside down and finally uncovered an arms cache. They hung up the unfortunate farmer by his hands and beat him up. When they let him down, he collapsed, on the verge of death. The despicable brutes loaded him onto a lorry, other hostages filled up other vehicles. Then the convoy moved off. The poor Resistance fighter soon died from his injuries. His corpse, forever silent, was of no more use to the great Germany. He was unceremoniously dumped by the side of the road. You can easily imagine the suffering of the unfortunate man's wife, who witnessed this unspeakable crime.'

A similar incident is referred to in several accounts given of a farmer being suspended from a beam in one of the outbuildings by his feet or by his hands and beaten during a raid at daybreak on 20–21 May 1944. The raid took place in Dévillac, neighbouring village to Lacapelle-Biron.[18]

....
18 https://www.ammacdufumelois.fr/articles.php?Ing=fr&pg=77
    Ammac is the *Anciens Marins et Marins Anciens Combattants du Fumélois*. The Association's website gives eyewitness accounts of what took place on 21 May 1944 during the raid on the villages of Vergt-de-Biron, Lacapelle-Biron, Gavaudan, Salles, Fumel, Monsempron, Mantagnac-sur-Lède, Frayssinet-le-Gélat.

Daughter Annie always affirms that her father was not part of the Resistance. 'Dad said he wasn't involved. He used to joke that he blew up a few bridges, but that was all.' It is clear from his memoir that he supported the activities of the maquis. In the following extract, Roland is waiting for their departure from Compiègne, along with the other prisoners. This would be their last stop on French soil. He expresses himself very forcefully:

'Then the next morning our departure was for real. Our first allocation was disrupted by the crush stupidly provoked by those who hung back the previous evening. Unfortunately, everyone suddenly wanted to react and to attempt the impossible. This meant the column which formed was a motley crew composed of an indiscriminate jumble of the pure and the impure, those who resisted from the beginning and those who had just joined (authentic Resistance fighters, and fighters since August or September). This last sentence will be understood by true Resistance fighters, of whom I was one, if not through my actions, then at least in my heart.'

Roland is referring here to those who claimed membership of the Resistance during those bitter years following the end of the war in Europe when French people were asking their neighbours and fellow countrymen and women 'What did you do in the war?' and meting out punishment to those who collaborated with the occupiers.

In his papers, Roland kept a *'Certificat de Présence au Corps'* date stamped November 1947, attesting to his membership of the Fumel Resistance group from 20 February 1943. He joined the Bataillon Geoffroy, Groupe Vény, part of the Forces Françaises de l'Intérieur (FFI) and was demobilised upon his return from Germany on 10 May 1945. The certificate states that Roland was deported by the Germans following a raid in the Fumel region, that he conducted himself admirably at all times and served the Resistance with *'Honneur et Fidélité'* (honour and loyalty).

The certificate was signed by Jean Vermont, former chief of the Bataillon Geoffroy, Groupe Vény, at the Mayor's office in Laneuville-à-Bayard in the Haute Marne department in the Champagne-Ardenne region.

Roland also kept a later certificate testifying to his membership of the FFI, date stamped Bordeaux, 26 September 1949. The certificate refers to Roland as a *déporté rapatrié* (returned deportee) and is signed on behalf of the military chief of staff.

The FFI is the name given to the French Resistance fighters in the later stages of the Second World War, used by Charles de Gaulle as a means of formalising their role as France changed from being an occupied nation to the status of a nation being liberated by the Allied armies.

•

GROUPES VÉNY

Resistance was a complex, multi-stranded, almost bureaucratic affair. The Groupes Vény grew out of the organisation of paramilitary groups in the Lot-et-Garonne region, originally part of the Armée secrète, the secret army. The Groupes Vény were named after their socialist leader, Jean Vincent, whose alias was Colonel Vény. The movement La France au combat (France in Action) divided the department into sectors, each one with its own divisional chief. These cells covered most of the area and were made up of the most trustworthy participants, *les hommes sûrs*. These groups would later form the framework of the Corps francs (military volunteer units).[19]

The Corps Francs de la Libération (CFL – volunteer freedom fighters) was the name given in May 1944 to all military aspects of the Mouvements Unis de la Résistance (MUR), the unified Resistance organisation in the southern zone, the unoccupied zone until the end of 1942. The MUR was set up in January 1943 as part of General de Gaulle's mission to streamline all the resistance forces. The CFL, however, gave way to the Forces Françaises de l'Intérieur as the true representation of co-ordinated armed Resistance. (Kedward, p. 300.)

By August 1944, the Groupes Vény were made up of four *bataillons* (battalions) or fighting units:
- Bataillon Geoffroy – Commander Vermont – this was the unit to which Roland belonged.
- Bataillon Jack – Commander Jacques Lévy
- Bataillon Georges – Commander Marrès
- Bataillon Corps francs de Casteljaloux – Commander Masson

---

19 http://www.cg47.org/archives/recherche/Bora/FRAD047_000000798.htm#CH1. Bora is the *Base d'orientation et de recherche archivistique*, part of the French public archives.

While the French Resistance was not a single movement, the term itself still conjures in the public imagination stories of courage and daring and awful suffering. As the Second World War recedes in our collective memories, Resistance remains an almost mythological 'brand'. This has been fed by cultural contributions – books, films and so on – that tell the stories of the Resistance fighters. It suited the post-war narrative that the French nation wanted to create about itself. The rawness of the reality of collaboration, antisemitism and self-interest was too much to bear.

This does not, of course, take anything away from the unimaginable courage it took resisters of all kinds to resist their invaders. Many of them were so very young. Their idealism and their youth must have provided a heady sense of invincibility in the face of so much fear, so much injustice and so much cruelty. Such resistance makes all of us question our own behaviour, makes us wonder how much courage, both moral and physical, each of us could muster when faced with such terror and fear.

And some eighty years on, Europeans may be nearer to having to ask themselves those questions again as the European Union witnesses the departure of a disintegrating UK, a decision that was voted for by only half the population, and the renewed outbreak of war on European soil. The invasion of Ukraine by the Russian state under the control of yet another brutish authoritarian is a demonstration of how the great European peace project remains essential to all of us. Ukraine is now resisting the occupiers; who might be next?

What is interesting is how few French people took an active role in the Resistance, although many of them may have died because of their association with, sympathy with, or even proximity to, those who were active participants. The instigation of the STO in 1943 was a significant spur to the thousands of young men who would have been deported to disappear into the countryside, not all of them to become *maquisards*, however. Some of them were happy to join the French paramilitaries, the Milice, policing their fellow citizens on behalf of the occupiers.

The Vichy regime had been allowed to maintain a French police force under the terms of the Armistice, which inevitably enabled collaboration between the French and their German rulers. Vichy was anti-Resistance, encouraging many young men, who had sympathy with the authoritarian beliefs of the Vichy regime, to join the Milice. Like all such paramilitary organisations, it succeeded in attracting all the usual suspects – the thugs and the fascists. (Paxton, p. 298.)

Paxton writes that after the war, some 300,000 Frenchmen received official veterans' status for active Resistance service: 130,000 as deportees and another 170,000 as Resistance volunteers. A further 100,000 died as a result of Resistance activity. The total of active Resistance participation at its peak adds up to about 2 per cent of the adult French population, according to official accounts after the war. However, others would have sympathised with the aims of the Resistance, willingly reading the underground newspapers produced in such dangerous circumstances and taking part in other peripheral aspects of resistance, writes Paxton. He calculates that some two million persons, or around 10 per cent of the adult population, might have taken this 'lesser risk'. (Paxton, pp. 294–295.)

Nevertheless, for the majority of French men and women, the risks of fighting, of openly defying the occupiers, were too great. (Paxton, pp. 294–5.) However much they longed for German occupation to end and for life to return to some semblance of normality, the choice was survival.

•

Daily life took different forms. People always find ways to adapt; they have to, whatever circumstances they are forced to endure – war, occupation, pandemics. Some never recover; some profit from others' suffering; some try rationally to live each day; some are overwhelmed. No one can tell ahead of time how they will be.

Certainly, most French people had to make the best of what they had, they had to manage somehow, they had to muddle through – this way of life, forced upon them, was known as *le système D* (as in *débrouillard* – resourceful), making do. The war years were a time of rationing and of shortages: of food (so many essential goods), of fuel (for both domestic heating and transport), of pleasures such as tobacco, of clothing, of housing (all that destruction, the lack of building materials). Imagine that for days, weeks, months on end, the most exciting element of your meal was a root vegetable: a swede – *un rutabaga*, a turnip – *un navet*, or the *pièce de résistance*, a Jerusalem artichoke – *un topinambour*.

The situation in France was not a uniform one – how could it be when one part of the country was occupied by the Germans and the other part unoccupied, at least until November 1942. City people scrimped and scrabbled differently from country people. Where Roland and Irène lived in the rural southwest, with its farms and land and animals, there was more to eat on the face of it. The movement of goods was strictly controlled, but people tried all manner of ruses to transport and exchange them. Amouroux writes of bottles of cognac and kilos of butter being smuggled through in the belly of a stuffed toy, for example, or of zealous inspectors suspiciously probing packages with a sharp instrument, sometimes with disturbing results. (Amouroux, p. 186.)

However, even if you had money, how could you buy goods and resources that simply were not available? The black market came into its own; at a time when the country thought of little else but food, just as Roland and his fellow deportees did in their captivity, everything was subject to barter and every deal was available. Everyone, from mothers to soldiers, from schoolchildren to fishermen, from postmen to grocers, was involved in this clandestine world and everyone had an angle. (Amouroux, p. 184.)

French civilians were assigned 1200 calories per adult per day in 1941, reduced to 900 calories in spring 1944.[20] Much of what France produced went to Germany. The Reich authorities selected France and Ukraine for increased grain exports to supply German civilians. There are echoes here of the situation in Ukraine in 2022. The invaders plunder the occupied country for supplies: the rule of the tyrant. During the war, the Germans made use of black markets to obtain stocks hoarded in the occupied zone and goods produced for French consumers in the unoccupied zone. Even when sellers did not want to supply the German occupiers with their goods, they would not necessarily know this was happening. The occupiers simply used intermediaries to make purchases in the southern zone and

---

20 Kenneth Mouré and Fabrice Grenard (December 2008). 'Traitors, "Trafiquants", and the Confiscation of "Illicit Profits" in France, 1944–1950'. *The Historical Journal*, Vol.15, No.4, pp. 969-990. Cambridge University Press

send them north across the demarcation line. These sellers would not know where their goods would end up.

•

CONTROLLING THE POPULATION

On top of all the deprivation and austerity and being hungry just about all the time, people were terrified of the reprisals.

If a German was shot, ten French citizens would be murdered in return. To support the Resistance was to put your life and the lives of your family on the line. Perhaps this persuaded Roland that 'blowing up one or two bridges' might be all that he could do to support those fighting the occupiers. He had a young family, a beloved wife, a baby son; he and Irène had a broad extended family. How easy would active resistance have been, when a single one of your actions could result in their destruction? He knows which side he is on; he also feels the heavy weight of risk and responsibility. This is not something he shared later on with his children as they were growing up nor even when they were adults. Like many others, he chose not to talk about his experiences, or if he did, he chose not to allow the weight of them to sit heavily on his family. Better to make light of what happened or to bury it.

•

THE TAKING OF LACAPELLE-BIRON

One of the villages standing in the way of the advance of the Reich division was Lacapelle-Biron.

The *réfractaires*, hiding out from the Vichy government-mandated programme of slave labour for Germany, and the maquis, the men and women trying to sabotage Germany's occupation of their country, became the targets of a massive pincer movement by the SS Reich division in what was a perfect storm of tragedy in May 1944 for the inhabitants of Lacapelle-Biron and surrounding villages. It was into this brutal, desperate mix that Roland was catapulted.

Lacapelle-Biron is a village in the Lot-et-Garonne department in southwestern France. It stands in the Lède valley on the edge of the region known as 'le Périgord noir', named originally for its dark oak forests. After the invasion and the division of France into occupied and unoccupied zones, Lacapelle-Biron was in the southern zone, under the authority of the Vichy government, until that ended in November 1942. To an extent, the southern zone had been somewhat spared, but not for everyone. People were always aware of the looming danger for anyone who had links with the Communist Party or for those who were engaged in Resistance activities. And even in such small communities as Lacapelle-Biron, there were refugees and people hiding for their lives, including Jewish families.

In Roland's memoir, he makes a handful of references to his 'luck':
'J'ai eu de la chance, j'ai eu de la chance.' (I was lucky.)

This always makes Annie laugh, because how could her father consider himself lucky in the circumstances? And yet she understands, for a handful of random decisions, a few acts of kindness, meant that he survived. There was solidarity among the deportees on the trains transporting them to the work camps, which meant they didn't try to cut each other's throats with pocketknives because there wasn't enough air for everyone to breathe. The deportees in his cramped and crowded wagon didn't fight as others in other wagons did, because there was no water and the heat was ferocious and the German soldiers were taunting them: 'You are resisters, so resist.' A woman in one of the work camps gave Roland extra rations of soup. An ordinary act but also extraordinary in its consequences – a stepping stone to an individual's survival.

However, on 21 May 1944, Roland Chopard was in the wrong place at the wrong time. The arrest was not because of any Resistance activities he may have engaged in, but because his luck, on this occasion, had run out.

•

It was dawn on Sunday 21 May 1944 when the heavily armed detachment from the SS Das Reich Division rolled into Lacapelle-Biron. This was just seventeen days before D-Day and the Allied landings in Normandy. The German army was slashing and burning as it moved northwards. The occupiers were on their way out after the complicated years of cruelty and accommodation with the occupants.

The German army's arrival was unheralded. The first that the inhabitants knew of what was happening was when soldiers turned up on their doorstep holding their machine guns in front of them, aimed at the person who opened the door.

They had blocked all the exits.

THREE

THE RAID ON LACAPELLE-BIRON

'Que reste-t-il aujourd'hui, au-delà du portrait figé sous verre qui ne me rappelle rien, et dans lequel je ne retrouve pas l'homme que j'ai appelé, si peu de temps, papa?'
('What is left now of the man I called Daddy, for so brief a time? Nothing but the photograph frozen in its frame.')

Marie-Claire Caumières

•

Marie-Claire Caumières, born Marmié, is one of a group of witnesses who took part in a film made in 2013 by the Association Mémoire Vive (Living Memory Association) in order to talk about their experiences one day in May 1944, the most terrible of days.[21]

What follows are stories from that day remembered by the people who lived through it, some of them not even five years old at the time. This was the day on which the life of the young Roland Chopard was turned upside down.

•

---

21 From *La Rafle au Coeur*. https://www.associationmemoirevive.com

LACAPELLE-BIRON, 21 MAY 1944

'*Tac, tac, tac.*'

Aline Chrétien, who was sixteen years old, remembers the sound made by boots stamping on the tiled floor as members of the SS Das Reich division raided her house. It was four o'clock in the morning of a spring day in the rural southwest of France.

'"Don't move," my dad said. "It's the Boches, stay in bed." I always remember the noise of the boots. They made the trees jump.'

•

The 2nd SS Das Reich Armoured Division had spent three years fighting on the Eastern Front. Arriving in southwestern France in the period before D-Day with the goal of controlling the disruptive *maquisards*, the behaviour of the soldiers was informed by their experiences in Russia. The same brutality was applied to the *résistants*, their supporters, and to entire villages. Reprisals against civilians were standard practice.

This was in the final stages of the Second World War just as the Allied invasion was about to happen. It felt like chaos. Germany was deploying its soldiers to spread terror and distrust. On 2 May, just under three weeks before the raid on Lacapelle-Biron, the SS retaliated to an attack on its soldiers by setting fire to several houses in Montpezat-de-Quercy and attacking civilians. In the following days, SS troops swept through the Lot department, rounding up people for deportation. Two women were shot in Cardaillac and one of them died. There was looting, assaults on property, general terror.[22] The SS Das Reich would subsequently go on to commit atrocities that ensure that its name continues to resonate among French people even today. The massacres that took place at Tulle[23]

---

22 Max Hastings (1983 paperback edition). *Das Reich: The March of the 2nd SS Panzer Division Through France, June 1944.* London: Pan Books Ltd.

23 On 9 June 1944, the SS Das Reich Division arrested men and boys between the ages of sixteen and sixty. Among these, ninety-nine were hanged on the same day, while 149 men were sent to Dachau concentration camp where the majority were murdered. https://tracesofwar.com/sights/13492/Memorial-Tulle-Massacre.htm

and Oradour-sur-Glane[24] after D-Day continue to exist in the collective memory as almost mythological examples of the extent to which humans can test the limits of their own barbarity.

Until the arrival of the SS Das Reich in their rural, rolling landscape, people in the southwest of France had been somewhat spared the ravages being endured in other parts of the country, according to local citizens who contributed to the *Mémoire Vive* film. Life went on in the usual way for many people, with restrictions and shortages but without daily terror. Nevertheless, there was an awareness of the growing danger for certain people – those who were supporters of the Communist Party or those who were engaged in Resistance activities. One witness speaks of her mother's two uncles being arrested in December 1943 in a neighbouring commune simply for belonging to the Communist Party. Vichy, of course, was terrified of communists and treated them as enemies of the state.

There was also awareness of the increasing danger faced by refugees, some Jewish, who were being hidden by some of the families in Lacapelle-Biron.

In the small hours of Sunday 21 May 1944, the SS Das Reich Division was given orders to hunt down the maquis through an area stretching from Villeneuve-sur-Lot to Frayssinet-le-Gélat (Lot).[25] The Division was stationed in Montauban in the Tarn-et-Garonne area, about 100km from Lacapelle-Biron.

The raid on Lacapelle-Biron was a purposeful, targeted attack, part of the occupying German army's intention to extinguish all remaining evidence of the French Resistance. Another witness, Michel Debiard, grandson of a deportee, is convinced of this.

'Everyone knew things were going badly for Nazi Germany,' says Debiard. 'This was just seventeen days before D-Day. No one knew about D-Day yet, but it was evident something was going on.'

It is plausible too that the refugees being sheltered in the village may also have been a target of the raid.

....

24 On 10 June 1944, the SS Das Reich Division killed 642 men, women and children in Oradour-sur-Glane before destroying the village. The ruins have been preserved. https://oradour.info
25 https://www.ammacdufumelois.fr/articles.php?Ing=fr&pg=77

Lacapelle-Biron was turned into *'une souricière'* (a mousetrap). Soldiers from the Das Reich division entered via the Gavaudun road and set up roadblocks. There were no exits.

•

'It was the *Fête des Mères*. I remember because Mum said we could have a lie-in.'

Jeannette Caminade was eight and a half years old when the Germans arrived at her house. She recounts the story as if she were still that small child, watching. The soft skin of her face is lit up with a procession of child-like expressions as she remembers.

'Then all of a sudden, I hear my mum saying to my dad, "I can hear the sound of engines," because around here you never heard such sounds. She gets up, she opens the window, "Oh but look, there are lorries coming up. I can see two. *Oh là, là,* one's stopping. They must be German lorries because they're green." Two Germans get out. They bang on the door. [Jeanette makes the noise of banging.] *Prang, prang, prang.*

'Mum opens the door and there are two Germans pointing their guns at her. [Jeannette mimes the soldier with the gun.]

'"Where is your husband?"

'"He's getting dressed."

'"Tell him to come here right away."

'"But wait, he's getting dressed."

'"But where is he, your husband?"

'So she leads them into the bedroom where we all are. My sister was in bed, I was standing. My little brother was still in bed. My mum signalled to me to get back into bed. So I do. The soldier insists.

'"Quick, quick, you have to go to the meadow down below Monsieur."

'"But he hasn't had any breakfast. He has to eat."

'"Oh no, no, no. When he comes back. When he comes back."

'The soldier points out of the window. "He has to go down there, into that meadow." Then he left. The other one went with him, through the gate.'

Jeannette says her dad saw them leave and decided to hide in the deep ditch outside where they would never find him. However, he had not reckoned on the loyalty of his dog. She came looking for him and would almost certainly have led the Germans to him. And if the Germans found him, they would certainly shoot him. He made the dog go away. Then he went to join the other men and boys in the meadow (where they were sent after being rounded up in the square).

'He had to,' Jeannette says simply.

•

Marie-Claire Caumières, an elegant woman wearing a bright pink scarf, was only four years and five months old when her father was taken away by the German army. Her family had a grocery shop in the town.

'I didn't recognise the language they were speaking. They searched all the rooms, went into the shop, took everything they fancied, rice, pasta… my mum was watching them, trying to stop them, but she couldn't. Dad wasn't there, I didn't see him leave. Then two men, two soldiers, went into the kitchen – my sister and I were there – one stood by the stove – I remember this very well – the other by the clock, on opposite sides of the room. We couldn't budge. The older one said to us, or rather whispered to us, he spoke French, "I also have two children about your age at home." I didn't know where that was.' (She shrugs, '*Bof*'.)

•

Denise Magnac, young wife of Louis Bugier, the butcher, was woken from sleep by an unusual noise. She peered out of the window and saw her neighbour talking to German soldiers in the road. He was in his shirtsleeves, which struck Denise as slightly unusual because it was still a bit fresh on those May mornings. She woke her husband, who moaned at her, said she should let him sleep, he was tired. He thought she was joking about Germans in the street.

He soon realised she wasn't joking.

They had already been talking for some time about how he should *filer au maquis* (hide out with the maquis) if a situation should occur such as the one taking place at that very moment. Her husband was the right age for the Service du Travail Obligatoire (STO) and was often sought by the local gendarmes but always managed to escape their clutches. Denise got a bag of provisions together and she and her husband and her young brother-in-law (he had turned eighteen just nine days ago) went out of the back of the house, intending to escape.

In the film, Denise is wearing a brown peaked cap on her still dark curls. It is easy to imagine her as a defiant young woman, facing up to the soldiers.

Too late. A German soldier was standing on the wall in front of them holding a machine gun. They had to return to the house.

More soldiers turned up. They went into the butcher's shop, started to raid the fridge. What was this white meat? *C'est quoi ça*? They had never seen such a meat before. They had no idea what veal was.

'I did a silly thing, I said it was "*une petite vache, eine kleine Küh*".'

That set the cat among the pigeons, why was she speaking German? Denise could not think of the German word for school, but finally they lost interest, waving away her words, '*Ja, Ja…*'

They continued to empty the fridge. Denise's husband was drinking his coffee, stirring in the sugar. 'Hurry up, you've got to join the others,' they said, 'in the main square.' Denise told her young brother-in-law René not to go; he was just eighteen but the soldiers didn't know that.

'But like all young men, he was proud to be eighteen. I couldn't hold him back. He went off with the others. He died in Belsen. *Voilà*.'

•

The SS were well informed, according to Michel Debiard. The Germans did not come to Lacapelle-Biron 'empty-handed' as the testimonies make clear. They knew which houses to go to. Certainly, the military police (*milice*) were everywhere – there were military police in Villeneuve and in Lacapelle. The witnesses mention the presence of two particular women. They had been living in the village for a while. A son of one of the women attended the local school. They often went to the post office, wrote letters to politicians like Pierre Laval, prime minister in the Vichy government and an advocate of closer cooperation with the Germans. On the very day of the roundup, the women left the village, they disappeared, and no one ever heard of them since then. Were they there to get the most exact details about the maquis, about life in the village, about the Jews who were hidden in some of the houses in the village?

'They knew everything,' says Aline Chrétien.

A house where the maquis were hiding had been set ablaze.

Debiard: 'We will never have any proof, but there are serious doubts casting their shadow.'

•

Yvette Delayre, the young wife of Jean Pericoli in May 1944, wears a bright shawl of pinks and greens, greys and whites. She remembers the day the Germans arrived as a morning like any other. But of course, it wasn't.

Yvette and Jean and Yvette's parents were all together. They talked of escape, but soldiers were everywhere with their machine guns. One soldier stood guard outside their house to prevent them leaving.

'All the soldiers were talking, talking... Thankfully they didn't come into the house. One of them asked me what one of the rooms was. "Oh it's just a store room." He didn't even come in. We were in the barn, cows behind us, hay. And underneath the hay there were barrels of petrol. They were kept there by the local resistance group [known as *le groupe Roland*]. They kept a parachute there which had been put there the evening before or the evening before that. They were going to take it the next day.'

•

Pierre Souchal, aged ten years, remembers the noise of the boots, of the engines, the motorbikes, how shocking it was.

'My grandmother was deaf, she didn't hear anything. We had to wake her up.'

One outstanding memory is of a woman with a drum who had climbed up onto a lorry and was announcing that all the men had to go to the main square. Pierre's father went on checking what was happening, going from house to barn to cellar, eventually to the square.

•

Throughout the day, the soldiers searched houses, barns, outbuildings – ransacking, terrorising. Their search spread to neighbouring villages where some people were tortured to death, others shot. In Lacapelle-Biron, witnesses like Pierre Souchal remember the sound of a drum being beaten. A woman, a clerk to the mayor *(appariteur)*, whose age varies between seventy-five and seventy-eight depending on the witness, was forced to get up onto a van which then was driven around the community. At each crossroads, she had to beat on the drum and announce that all the men should gather immediately in the main square.

In the square, the seventy-one-year-old mayor Monsieur Lagarrigue used the electoral register to call the names of all the men in the village. Sixty men, including the priest Roger Dané, were then herded together in a meadow in the custody of soldiers bearing machine guns.[26]

•

Jeannette Caminade remembers the priest being arrested.

'We used to spend every day looking out of the glass front door. That day we were looking out over the meadow. [Jeannette waves her hand to indicate the field where she is standing and where the men and boys were herded.]

'They [the Germans] kicked them, some fell over, they hadn't eaten. My father was among them. He went with them. We didn't see him. We would have liked to see him, we were really upset, especially as… [she shakes her head].

'They arrested the priest, but then they let him go. He said, "They are my parishioners, I will stay with them." "No, no, no, you can stay." He insisted. On the lorry – my mum saw him get onto the lorry – and they were saying, "No, no stay here." He refused. He insisted on staying with his parishioners. "I will follow them. Where they go, I will go."

'They even took the dog, poor thing.'

....
26 https://www.ajpn.org/commune-Lacapelle-Biron-47123.html
    (AJPN=*Anonymes, Justes et Persécutés durant la période Nazie dans les communes de France;* The Nameless, Righteous and Persecuted during the Nazi period in French communities.)

•

Sitting on the bench outside the grey stone wall of her house, Aline Chrétien recounts a story.

'There was a man from Alsace, a young man, eighteen years old, who told us he had been taken by force by the Germans. "Look at what I've got," he said, and showed us a *torche* [flame thrower] for setting things alight. He had a machine gun on his back, or something, I don't know. He said, "If ever the maquis come, I will use a *torche* to set the village on fire." "There aren't any maquis here," we told him. "That's for sure, there aren't any maquis." Because we were frightened that he might accuse us. Yet there were some, around, in the woods.' [Aline gestures behind her with her hands, as if maquis might still be there, hiding out in the dense undergrowth.]

'He told us not to stay outside standing there, to go home, to go indoors, because someone might take a shot at us.'

•

Alsace and Lorraine in the northeast of France had been annexed by Germany and placed under German administration as part of the Reich. Those who fled could not return home. It was forbidden. The rest of northeastern France was sealed off and populated with German settlers who took over 'abandoned' farms so that refugees could not return there. The Armistice was supposed to be a temporary arrangement, yet by October 1940 all natives of Alsace and Lorraine were no longer allowed to be part of the Armistice army permitted under Vichy, nor the Chantiers de la Jeunesse. And those Lorraine natives who wanted to keep French citizenship were forced to leave. Refugees flooded into France, joining all of those who were desperately fleeing the northern towns and cities and moving south. (Paxton, pp. 55–56, p. 362.)

Many young *Alsaciens* were forced into the German army or into the SS divisions. Some of the witnesses mention that some of the soldiers involved in the raid spoke French. These young *Alsacien* soldiers were known as *'les malgré-nous'* – 'the in-spite-of-ourselves' – French speakers compelled to join the German army.

•

Jacques Augié was aged five years, eight months when the Germans came. When he recounts the events of that day, it is as if he is inhabiting that small boy's body again, reliving those moments of a child's horror as everything familiar is turned upside down. His father Abel Augié was a baker and ran the mill at Courrances.

'That morning, very early, I was still in bed when the door to my room was opened and two frightening-looking people rushed into the room, went towards the wardrobe. One of them took out a drawer, tipped it up and dumped it at the foot of the bed. Then he opened the wardrobe's other door and rummaged around amongst the sheets and the over blankets and what-not, obviously to see whether there were any hidden arms (and certainly we were right to think that, as we found out later).

'Then the one on the right left the room while the other continued coming round my bed and dug around in the small night table on the right side of my bed. He even pulled out the drawer and dumped that one too at the foot of the bed. He even got down on his knees to look under the bed to see if there was anything hidden there. And I was still on the edge of my bed, on the bolster, terrified, and I even remember that I was dribbling with terror. And when this man got back up, something extraordinary happened. He looked at me. It seemed to me that that was the first time he really looked at me. He came towards me, he even passed his hand across my forehead, he said something that I didn't understand but which seemed to mean "This is none of your doing, little one." Then he went out again by the door which gave onto the dining room next door, and I stayed there, flat out for a moment, and instinctively I looked towards the window which looked out onto the garden in the back onto the little river, known as the Lède.

'The day was just dawning. I got up from my bed – because I was all alone – and I went towards the door which connected with the dining room and at the very moment I stepped through this door, I saw opposite me, framed against the backdrop of the rising sun, the face of Marcelle Magnac. Marcelle was my nanny, my babysitter in a way. She was signalling though the window: leave, leave.

'Her face, as I looked at her through the window, stays engraved on my mind.'

•

MARCELLE

A black and white picture of Marcelle at eighteen shows a beautiful young woman with a tiered mass of dark hair wearing bright earrings. When she speaks to the camera, it is possible to get a sense of her eighteen-year-old self.

'I was staying over at Pauline's house. The Germans woke us up and on my way home, I went past Jacques' house and told him: "Get out, get out." There were Germans everywhere, I had to go and warn my parents. When I got to Jacques' house, I heard some noise in the *fournil* [bakery], because the Germans were already there and were in the process of arresting Abel [Jacques' dad].'

•

JACQUES

'Once Marcelle had gone, I was again all alone in what was the dining room and immediately afterwards, I heard muffled sounds coming up from under the floor, from the *fournil* where my dad was working, the noises were getting louder and louder. They were coming towards the outside stone staircase. A few moments later, my mum and my brother came through the door which overlooks the pond and found me there. My brother stood in the corner by the door, sobbing [Jacques is almost crying at this point]. My mum took me in her arms and came to sit down on a chair – here [he indicates the place] – she said, "Daddy had to go to Lacapelle." That reassured me a bit. Mum was holding me tight. My gaze alighted on some vases which stood on the fireplace mantelpiece opposite. And since then, I've never been without these three vases.'

He indicates them, standing on top of a glass-fronted cupboard – they are of a shiny brown ceramic, decorated with green streaks as if dripping down the sides.

Abel Augié died in captivity.

•

MARCELLE

She is standing outside a grey stone farmhouse.

'I made it home from Jacques' house to warn my parents that the Germans were here, then I warned my brother who was nineteen years old.' He went off into the woods. Marcelle says this with pride that she saved him.

The Germans came in through the gate, saying in French, *'Perquisition, perquisition.'* They rummaged everywhere, taking jewellery from the chest of drawers. Marcelle indicates a place on the wall where a map of Germany was hanging. She remembers that her dad pointed to a spot on the map and told the Germans, 'My son is there,' which seemed to please them 'that he had a son in Germany who worked for them.'

Marcelle continues, 'But we were frightened because of the guns,' and she gestures towards the top of the wardrobe. 'My dad hadn't wanted to give up his guns, which were hidden in the *corniche* of the wardrobe. So our hearts were beating hard. We knew the guns were there.'

The tension was broken after a long moment, by the Germans demanding lunch, which Marcelle's mother made for them: some ham and an omelette.

'They drank, ate and when they had finished, one of the Germans said to my dad:

'"How old are you?"

'"I'm fifty-five years old."

'"Fifty-five? Say you're sixty, you haven't shaved, they're arresting all the men under sixty, they would arrest you."'

Marcelle says it was a man from Alsace who saved her dad. 'And my brother had gone off into the woods, fortunately, because he would have been arrested as he was nineteen.'

•

How sad that it was raining, the nine-and-a-half-year-old Christiane Marmié was thinking when the Germans arrived.

'Mum said the Germans are here.'

They were violent, threatening. Christiane remembers very clearly – *'un souvenir précis'* – falling to her knees to pray that no harm would befall them.

'My dad came up to me, hugged me – for the last time. Mum wanted Dad to hide, go to the next village, seek refuge. But he feared reprisals against his family, so he joined others in the square.'

•

Denise Magnac's family had reason to be fearful. They hid the Jewish George Rosenthal through the winter from October the previous year until March 1944.

The young Denise knew what was at stake when she was questioned by 'a great big man, with piercing, wicked eyes, even just seeing him like that, you could tell…'

He had already interrogated her mother, asking her if she was Mme B. Denise's mother had denied this. Obviously it was a case of mistaken identity. They had a Jewish neighbour who was a bit stocky, the same body shape as Denise's mum, and who had white hair, also like Denise's mum.

'Mum kept saying, "No, I'm not Mme B." She had to go fetch her ID card, prove her identity. A few moments later, he saw me, "You're Jewish." "No, I'm not Jewish," I said. And he followed me into my bedroom to get my ID card.'

•

Five-and-half-year-old Josette Da Costa was at home on the family farm, about 2km from Lacapelle, when the Germans came. The geese were cackling in the yard. Mum told the soldiers that her husband was cutting grass for the cows in the field right next door. A soldier followed them to the field, but, 'My dad wasn't there any more because he had already heard the noise over at the neighbour's, got a bit frightened and took off into the woods. So the Germans asked my mother what nationality her husband was, she replied, "He's Portuguese," and they said, "If we find him, we will hang him."'

•

Reprisals were a useful weapon for fighting the Resistance. In the Lot region, there was great cooperation between the *maquisards* and the locals. Several of the witnesses mention their fear that guns would be discovered as the soldiers entered their houses, their barns, freely searched their land, their property, put their hands on every possession, every item of food or drink. By 1944, the pretence of any kind of autonomy had disappeared with the occupation of the Vichy 'free zone'; people were being forced to make choices about where their loyalties – and interests – lay. Those who supported Marshal Pétain, many of them survivors of the First World War for whom the Marshal remained an admirable figure, were being challenged by the younger generation, who had choices of their own to make. (Kedward, p. 127.)

Throughout the day, as people's houses and outbuildings were searched, as the soldiers demanded food and ate eggs and ham cooked by the women, and as children became more bewildered and the adults more fearful, there still was no full realisation of what was to come. Women were concerned for their husbands, sons, fathers, brothers who were being guarded in a field, deprived of food and drink. Some tried to take supplies to them, but it wasn't easy.

Some of the younger men took off into the woods, sleeping rough, waiting it out.

'We thought stupidly that the raid was to check IDs, to round up labour for the STO, to get provisions. We were very naïve, not at all informed,' said Denise Magnac.

•

By six in the evening, the Germans had sorted the men according to age and those between eighteen and sixty were being rounded up in the main square, usually the location for a game of *pétanque,* and loaded into lorries.

The lorries drove away forty-nine men from Lacapelle.

Pierre Souchal did not witness the exact moment that his dad went to the square. Pierre was ten years old. He remembers the women worrying that the men would be cold, all stuffed into the lorries. Someone gave him a book of poetry to distract him.

The farewells were very quick, all too quick. Men climbing into the lorries, men standing around to the right, to the left. It felt heartbreaking, *'un déchirement',* literally a tearing apart.

The SS took them along the road heading to Gavaudun. They stopped at the Hôtel des Roches at Majoulassy, where other prisoners were added to the captured *Capelains*. This was probably where Roland Chopard joined them. At around seven o'clock, the 118 raid victims were on their way to the Toussaint barracks at Agen. This was the start of their journey to the Dachau and Mauthausen camps.

Of the forty-nine taken from Lacapelle, twenty-six returned from the camps. Some of the survivors died in the year following their return. Of the 118 deportees, fifty-two would die on German soil.

•

Marie-Claire Caumières was born to the Marmiés on 26 December 1939. (For me, this is poignant as it is exactly fifty years to the day before the birth of my own daughter, writer and teacher Lily Peters.) Marie-Claire too trained as a teacher. One morning, she was sitting in her classroom waiting for her pupils to arrive. She had a sudden irrepressible urge to write an account of the day her father was taken, leaving behind his family, his girls, unaware that they would never see each other again. This was before the creation of the Living Memory Association.

This is what she wrote:

'I had been going to school in Lacapelle for a few weeks since the beginning of the Easter term. I didn't like school much and yet I would be taking that same path to school for the next fifty years.

'Today, 21 May 1944, there is no school. It's Sunday, Mother's Day *(la fête des mères)*, and my sister and I were eager to give Mum the present that we had been making secretly.

'I got up and then... nothing. I no longer knew anything at all about the present, not what it was nor where it was hidden. All I could see in the house, on the staircase, in my bedroom, were men in uniform, in their boots, in their helmets, digging through everything and taking whatever they pleased in spite of Mum's angry looks. Dad was already gone. And two other men, soldiers, Nazis (I didn't yet know that word) – one young one with a fierce look and an older one who looked friendlier, who made sure we stayed still, my sister near the clock and me near the cooker.

'It felt like this lasted the whole day. Such a heavy silence, unbearable stillness.

'And then it was the end of the afternoon and we found ourselves in the street directly in front of Cazal's garage. There were Germans everywhere, lorries, armed soldiers yelling orders that I couldn't understand and I could see men from our neighbourhood, men I saw everyday: Gilbert and René who often lifted me up into their arms; our neighbour Roland who loved teasing me; François who worked at our house; the vicar… and then, my dad and everyone else crammed into lorries.

'We stood there, we three, Mum, Christiane and me, amongst the terrified women and children, powerless and unable to imagine the unimaginable.

'The convoy set off. I will never forget this green-grey convoy. I watched it right up until it rounded the bend in the valley.

'It was over. I understood nothing and in a few hours, my universe was turned upside down. I would never again see my dad.

'What is left now of the man I called Daddy, for so brief a time? Nothing but the photograph frozen in its frame.

'We watched them until they went round the first bend in the valley. Then it was over. I didn't have any proof that he died. We just waited. It was a terrible absence that lasted all my life.'

Raoul Marmié died in Dachau.

•

ROLAND IS TAKEN…

While the raid was taking place, Roland was not actually in Lacapelle-Biron but on his bike on the way to his aunt's house in Monflanquin.

In an interview with *La Dépêche du Midi* in November 2016,[27] the eighty-seven-year-old Roland described how he was taken:

---

27 *La Dépêche du Midi* (29 November 2016). Translated by the author. https://www.ladepeche.fr/article/2016/11/29/2468077-rendre-l-histoire-plus-proche-et-garder-la-memoire-vive.html

'J'étais parti au ravitaillement du côté de Lacapelle, chez ma tante. Je suis tombé en pleine rafle, en mai 1944, au moment de l'épisode tragique des villageois victimes de la barbarie...' (I had set out for my aunt's place near Lacapelle to get food supplies. I got caught up in the middle of a raid in May 1944 at the very moment of the tragedy befalling the villagers, victims of savagery…)

He was taken just two weeks before D-Day on 6 June 1944, when Allied forces launched their assault on Nazi-occupied France.

FOUR

THE CAPTURE

The weather was unsettled on the morning of Sunday 21 May 1944. While people in Lacapelle-Biron were being terrorised and their homes ransacked by soldiers from the SS Das Reich division, Roland Chopard was setting off on his bike from his home in Fumel towards Monflanquin where his aunt lived.

He was on his way there in search of fresh food supplies, by way of Lacapelle.

Roland was twenty-seven years old, a personable young man with his dark hair slicked back from his forehead and the strong flexible body of a man who loves sports. He had always loved sports, ever since he could remember. It was the thing that helped him to endure a childhood and adolescence that was quite unsettled, if not all that unusual at the time.

Roland's father, Alexandre, was the youngest of four boys born to Pierre Chopard and his wife. They also had a daughter, Léa. Roland did not know either Pierre or his grandmother very well while he was growing up; this was to be the pattern of his childhood.

In notes he made on his family history, Roland wrote that his father Alexandre followed in the footsteps of his brothers, receiving limited schooling and going out to work in the fields from the age of ten. The family lived in Toutry in the Bourgogne region, located in the Côte d'Or department. Luckily for the inquisitive and smart Alexandre, the Schneider du Creusot[28] metalworks had a branch locally and the boy was able to take up a professional apprenticeship there. The company was a major arms manufacturer in the Second World War.

As a qualified craftsman, Alexandre was able to undertake the traditional tour of France doing work placements with master craftsmen, under the auspices of the Compagnons du Devoir[29] organisation, first established back in the Middle Ages. The tour didn't just teach professional skills to young men (and the *compagnons* were all male at that time) but also how to live independently and get along with people.

Roland describes his father as an impulsive traveller, thirsty to enlarge his horizons, but Europe at that time was a land of closed borders, so he chose Morocco in northwest Africa, before the First World War came to disrupt everyone's lives. That choice informed his whole life and the lives of his children. Indeed, Roland was to return to West Africa, to Sénégal, after the Second World War to make his living there and to support his family. He and Irène made the same choices for their children as Roland's father made for his children – sending them back to France for their education at an extremely young age.

Like most children, Roland enjoyed stories of his father's youthful adventures and admired his resourcefulness. In particular, he relates how Alexandre found a comfortable hideout as a cook in the officers' mess, where he rubbed shoulders with senior officers.

Alexandre had been called up and had to use all his skills to find for himself such a satisfactory position – *'Oh combien fructueuse.'* It meant he had room to manoeuvre.

Roland writes:

'I'll just mention one incident he told us about. Looking for wine, he and a mate went down to the dockside at a port where barrels of wine were stored. He managed to pierce one of them to pour off a few bottles'

---

28 Schneider-Creusot was originally an iron and steel business, becoming a major arms manufacturer. https://www.musee-orsay.fr/en/events/exhibitions/in-the-museums/exhibitions-in-the-musee-dorsay/article/les-schneider-le-creusot-une-famille-une-entreprise-une-ville-1836-1960-4142.html?cHash=b0146337fd
29 *Compagnons du Devoir et du Tour de France* is a French organisation of craftsmen and artisans first established in the Middle Ages. https://en.wikipedia.org/wiki/Compagnons_du_Devoir; https://www.bbc.co.uk/news/world-europe-42365048

worth. An officer appeared, was summarily put out of action and our two rascals went back to their base with their precious stash. But back at base, there was general commotion: troops being assembled, a detailed review. The officer who had been assaulted had to find these hooligans, but they weren't present, because being part of the kitchens, they weren't among the *"bidasses ordinaires"*, the ordinary grunts. *"Donc, affaire classée"*, the affair was filed away.'

Alexandre's life was fully intertwined with the French colonial presence in the African continent. While the timings are not clear, it seems he took part in the Battle of Rif in Morocco, some years after the end of the Great War. He was living in Morocco then, having married Rose Euphreusine, a *Pied-Noir*[30] woman from Morocco, and moving there after the war to try his luck in a variety of occupations. (Annie remembers with joy her grandmother's fantastic couscous, *'un couscous merveilleux'*.)

Roland was born in Oujda, located in the northeastern corner of Morocco, near the border with Algeria.

•

THE BATTLE OF RIF

The background to this battle in Morocco, at that time a French protectorate, is complex, but essentially involves the colonial powers of France, Spain and Britain going to war with the Rif, the collective term for the Berber groups who inhabited the harsh mountainous terrain.

The French became involved in 1925 and, interestingly, Philippe Pétain, the 'Hero of Verdun' and later the head of the Vichy collaborationist government, was appointed general-in-chief of the French Moroccan forces. The conflict ended in May 1926. It was a brutal period – 43,500 Spanish troops killed, missing or wounded, 18,000 French troops, and Rif losses estimated at 30,000 casualties, with 10,000 deaths. Among them were probably many Rif civilians, who had been subjected to poison gas bombs as well as the conventional kind.[31]

....
30 Pieds-Noirs are Europeans who lived in Algeria for generations but left the country with the colonial administration.
31 See https://www.britannica.com/event/Rif-War.

True to form, Alexandre tried out a variety of different occupations and found himself caught up in some wild incidents. One of Roland's stories concerns Alexandre's stint as a lorry driver. This was not a very safe job. The roads were full of twists and turns with pockmarked stony surfaces, while the fear of being attacked by the locals was ever-present. The lorries of the day were very rudimentary with cabs open to the weather, so they were equipped with a driver's assistant and potentially a guard dog, both uncomfortably installed on the piles of goods.

Alexandre was not a man to be deterred by any mechanical breakdown. He knew his way around an engine.

Roland writes:

'And one fine day, the attack came. A man jumped on to the footstep brandishing a knife and tried to kill the driver; but the driver, still on the alert, managed to push off the assailant and continued on the road. When he arrived, he found the weapon, *un poignard* [a dagger], on the back seat. This was one of the reasons that may have persuaded him to abandon this dangerous occupation, as well as a few financial setbacks caused by a few dodgy debtors.'

After these adventures and as the war receded into the background, Alexandre finally decided to settle his family in, what was called at the time, French West Africa, where he became an overseas civil servant, based in the port town of Abidjan, capital of the *Côte d'Ivoire*.

Roland seems quite clear-sighted about his father. In his notes, he writes that, 'This *"personnage hors du commun"* [this unusual person] now seemed to acquire some of the wisdom that had completely evaded him up until this point.'

•

Annie remembers her funny grandfather, his adventures, his knack of managing to escape tricky situations. Evidently, these are stories that have been passed along through the generations. Annie's brother was named for their grandfather: 'Mum said that when Alex was born, Roland went to register him at the *Mairie*. She wanted him to be called Alain. She chose Alain and another name – perhaps it was Alexandre, to make the grandfather happy.'

However, when Roland arrived at the *Mairie*, the official there said that only one single first name was permitted. 'He chose Alexandre – "that'll make Dad happy."'

'I remember Mum saying: *"Quand j'ai vu le petit bout de chou, oh Alexandre."'* Both Irène and Roland agreed that the name was too long for this tiny scrap, so they used to call him *'le titounet'* ('the little one' in patois) which became shortened to *'Titou'*. They continued to tease him with this as he grew, *'Titou, Titou, Alex'*.

'It's better than Alain anyway,' Annie adds, chuckling.

•

Roland's childhood was flavoured by its African beginnings, but he was only there for a short time before he and his older sister were packed off to boarding school in France as was the tradition in colonial families. A long time afterwards, as an adult, Roland wrote of the harshness of the climate and of the conditions of living that did not lend themselves to the education of young children. In this, he didn't move on much from the beliefs of his own parents. When he, in turn, decided to decamp with his family to Sénégal to make a life there after the dreadful experience of the war and of living under occupation, the children Annie and Alexandre were sent off to France for their schooling too. But that is in the future.

Roland was thus quite used to being on his own, able to take stock of a situation and think about how to manage it. A child of his time, he was self-sufficient and temperamentally stable, not easily frightened.

When he was riding his bike towards Monflanquin, a day later than he had originally planned, he was not unusually nervous.

•

Roland liked his aunt Léa Giraudeau, his dad's sister. He used to spend his summers with her when he was at boarding school because his parents were in West Africa. Annie remembers her as rather smart, rather lovely.

'People warned him that there were Germans in the area.' Annie makes a gesture as if washing her hands, a decisive gesture: 'Pop, pop, pop. I'm going anyway!' She is imitating her dad. 'Food was more important.'

Living in an occupied country means nothing can be trusted, nothing is certain, but nevertheless Roland was not expecting what happened next.

•

FROM ROLAND'S MEMOIR

It was raining on that Saturday, 20th of May. I couldn't go out on my bike for fresh supplies, as I usually did, so I put off this practical outing until the next day. The night was calm and I slept peacefully. The never-ending monotony of the traffic noise, even though it was very unusual and obtrusive, did not wake me. Of course, I lived some distance from the main road. When I got up I made my final preparations, armed myself with a knapsack, a snack, some paper in which to wrap the eggs I was hoping to find, and set off for a destination 20km away, believing that I would return that evening or, at the latest, the next morning, if the weather, which was unsettled as I was leaving, were to turn rainy.

I was several kilometres away from my objective. I had been overtaken by several Jerry military vehicles, including one armoured car. Carefree and still ignorant of Nazi methods, my imagination wasn't stirred by this encounter. And so, I continued on my way, happy to breathe the open air of the countryside and cheered up by the comforting spectacle of nature coming back to life. The winding road sloped downwards. I rode on without breaking a sweat and soon arrived at the last bend at the bottom of this long incline.

My heart gave a sudden lurch at the sight of a Jerry roadblock, set up next to a small bridge, about 100 metres in front of me.

My first thought was to turn around. But this thought had been anticipated by our accursed and evil (I only realised this later) occupiers. A Kraut armed with a machine gun had been stationed at a dip in the road, slightly hidden by a shrub and immediately after the bend, and thus invisible to anyone following my itinerary. I was forced to present myself at the roadblock.

'Papiere?' was the only question put to me. I decided to comply. As luck would have it, I was carrying all my IDs [identity papers]. I was patted down summarily but pointlessly; my aim on that day was a peaceful one. Then I was shown with a gesture what direction to follow. It wasn't the

same one of course. In this spot near the road, the rocky wooded hills formed a sort of clearing where it was easy to gather together lots of people and keep them under surveillance. On the pathway leading to the clearing, many lightweight cars and a few lorries were parked. The 'field-greys' [referring to uniforms of the German soldiers] came and went, indifferent to the civilians being rounded up in the designated area. I walked about 100 metres, wheeling my bike, and found myself among several fellow countrymen, most of them local peasants. I went over to a wall to lean my bike against it, then I looked around the immediate surroundings which I would have found picturesque in any other circumstances. Here and there, some openings led out onto the wide fertile countryside all around, but I also saw a soldier with hair that stood up like a hedgehog's, wearing a dirty green uniform, looking like a beast and as still as a statue.

This was not a time to be cocky. But really, what was there to fear? My inexperienced judgement allowed me to hope there would be a peaceful conclusion to this unlawful open-air detention.

'They'll check our identities,' I thought, 'then they'll let us go, or most of us.'

Most of my companions were decent countrymen, harmless and still completely bewildered by this arbitrary arrest.

'Well, let's wait and see,' I said. Our group expanded by one or two as women too suffered the same fate as us. Time passed. Soon, the noon angelus bell rang out from the church in the neighbouring village. Our group became a gathering. A rain shower increased the growing unease. Meanwhile, people I knew had come to join me. We discussed the reasons for this roadblock and found out that it was only one part of a vast roundup organised in the surrounding area. Then our thoughts turned to other more comforting subjects. It was very late in the day when an officer approached us accompanied by a German woman, his interpreter – actually, a very bad interpreter.

The ID checks we had been hoping for over the past ten hours started. The women were let go, some old people too. An epileptic man who had suffered a seizure during the day was also released. Poor wretch, probably a day labourer, dragging his misery from one farm to another. The rest of us (for from now on what were we and what would become of us?) were forced to sit down, side by side on the ground in tightly packed rows.

At either end of this miserable human anthill, a Kraut, holding a rifle, surveyed us cynically. Then the order to stand up was given. We had to maintain our rows. We were told to empty our pockets completely and throw the contents on the ground. It was soon strewn with cigarettes, despite the great shortage, with matches and lighters and with all sorts of sundry and unexpected objects.

The greedy Krauts quickly made their choice. Even so, they feared being seen by their superiors. No doubt, in their subconscious, they believed this venal act unworthy of their people, but their military education as Nazis had snuffed out in them any idea of human dignity. The German soul, rotten, brutal, war-like, slightly mitigated perhaps by the beneficial effect of neighbouring civilisations, had suddenly burst forth freely with the reign of Hitler. That evening, the guards closest to us had an ample harvest of various objects, but especially of the thing so dear in both senses of the word – our tobacco.

A little later, a lorry arrived, then a second one. The pickings from other roundups got out of the lorries. The gathering was impressively large. And the way we were handled grew more disciplined as a result. We were divided into three groups, carefully counted and led over to the big, covered lorries where we were stuffed in like sardines. The tightly tied-down tarpaulins partitioning the lorries meant we couldn't enjoy for one last time the uplifting view of the sun setting over the lush and leafy countryside.

We were able to figure out the route we were taking through tiny holes in the tarpaulins. We travelled about 60 kilometres before reaching the main town of the department. There, we were driven into a barracks. The lorries drew up and we got out. Night had fallen. More guards joined our escort. The contents of each lorry were counted once again by the dim light of the hurricane lamps. There were hoarse angry yells. Then in columns of three we were led towards a drill hall which appeared to have been abandoned a long time ago. Our new masters showed us the side we were to sleep on. The opposite side served as the toilets. We hurried first to relieve ourselves, then to find a place for some restorative rest, although it was more of a troubled sleep, pierced through with hellish visions and Dantesque nightmares. The breaking of the day didn't exactly surprise us; we were all awake. From the early hours, many of us had been woken by the cold and had got up to warm ourselves by pacing back and forth.

Little by little the daylight illuminated our strange prison. An earth floor, made of sawdust and dung, high walls surmounted with windows and a vast roof. The fresh morning air seemed icy on our skin after a night of insomnia and a day without food. The comings and goings of those who were more sensitive to the cold had kicked up a cloud of dust. Finally, the full day dawned and with it the hope of better tomorrows.

We continued to talk about the massive arrest, but this time there were several arguments, then we were overcome by our physical needs and sought out something to eat. Most of us hadn't eaten anything since yesterday morning. Our guards told us that the local Red Cross had been informed and would provide us with food.

The day was long, and even more so because we were hoping that a more thorough interrogation would give us a clearer idea of our fate, but the hours passed. While we waited, the sun had heated up the air and soon it was hot. During the afternoon, many of us stretched out and slept. Finally, towards evening, the Red Cross arrived. There was quite a crush, but everyone managed at last to get their meagre ration. We found out about the number of meals daily and were slightly comforted by the promise of two meals. We awaited the second night. We had settled into our quarters in as clean a way as possible (or perhaps I should say in the least dirty way), and the second night went by just like the first despite our rustic arrangements. Left to myself finally in the relative silence of the improvised dormitory, under the unrelenting surveillance of a machine gun mounted on a table at the entrance (for from now on it couldn't be an exit – what happened subsequently would teach me that, unfortunately), I reflected on this adventure that I couldn't yet describe as tragic.

•

I was most unhappy about how upset my family would be when they received this sad news. I was in no doubt at all that news of this Nazi expedition would have been all over the neighbouring area within the space of a single day. Sure enough, my absence on Sunday evening made my wife suspicious. But she considered the changeable rainy weather was good enough reason for my staying the night at my aunt's. First thing the next morning, my wife telephoned our relative about me. My aunt said that I had not been at her house. The light dawned immediately. My wife's suspicions were confirmed and the small town where I lived soon learned that the travellers who had set off the day before and who were expected home the next day or even that same evening, but who didn't show up, had fallen prey to the Krauts.

Then all hell broke loose as false news, always more alarming than the truth, started to circulate. My family had to hear terrifying versions of my fate. Beaten, tortured, maimed – and ultimately, shot for rebellion. These apparently overblown accounts could be explained by the atrocities that had taken place a few months earlier in an area nearby, memories of which were now suddenly resurfacing in people's minds. My family had to suffer all this speculation. Then the local authorities issued the correct information and serenity reigned again once our whereabouts were known.

Yet this Nazi expedition could not help leaving traces of blood on its way. In an insignificant country village, a farmer had been denounced as being in possession of weapons. The Krauts seized him and used multiple threats to try to get him to admit links with the local Resistance. Faced with his denials, they turned his house upside down and finally uncovered an arms cache. They hung up the unfortunate farmer by his hands and beat him. When they let him down, he collapsed, on the verge of death. The despicable brutes loaded him onto a lorry, other hostages filled up other vehicles. Then the convoy moved off. The poor Resistance fighter soon died from his injuries. His corpse, forever silent, was of no more use to the great Germany. He was unceremoniously dumped by the side of the road. You can easily imagine the suffering of the unfortunate man's wife, who witnessed this unspeakable crime.

Our numbers swelled. Soon our curiosity was aroused by the arrival of a passenger car in which we could see a civilian, his hat pulled down low, the collar of his coat turned up. Very quickly however our curiosity gave way to pity when we saw the body of a man, covered with a blanket, being pulled from the car. We saw traces of blood at the level of his pelvis. We assumed that a burst of machine gun fire had stopped him as he fled. He was dumped on the ground and left there without treatment of any kind. He was groaning and calling for something to drink. A woman from a nearby house came to bring him a glass of water. An officer sent her back abruptly. Confronted with our utter helplessness we turned away from this depressing sight. Several people thought they recognised the civilian. As for me, I simply thought of him as one of those despicable men who sold out to our enemies for a paltry sum.

•

The pale dawn light of the second day illuminated the nocturnal walkers who were fighting the cold's grip as they had the day before, by repeatedly pacing back and forth. Soon, everyone was awake and on their feet. We were getting filthier and the lack of water made it difficult to clean ourselves properly. We carefully saved the few buckets of water we received each day to quench our thirst. The lack of wine was also debilitating. Most of us really appreciated the alcohol which would have been of great benefit to us, especially during these feverish days. (And yet we still got soup on time that day.) During the morning, we had a visit from several Krauts in civilian dress. We were counted for the umpteenth time and there was a roll call. A short interrogation followed, reduced to a handful of questions about our likely ties with the maquis and what we knew about the Resistance.

Most of them, incapable unfortunately of making any move towards freedom, some committed collaborators, and a minority who were active Resistance fighters, everyone, whether honest or crafty, declared themselves ignorant of the questions being put to them. Unfortunately, some among us had been victims of denunciations, while others had been arrested in circumstances that the Krauts found compromising and connected (very likely) to the Resistance. Those who fell into these two categories were suspects and, as such, were to be subjected to a special, individual interrogation.

These compromising circumstances need to be described in detail. They prove, backed up by thousands of other examples, that the judgement of these would-be masters of the universe was stupid and defective.

One suspect had been arrested while he was riding on his motorbike – on his moped, to be exact. He was on his way to the butcher's in the neighbouring village. The use of petrol on a Sunday morning could not be explained legally. They didn't understand the completely truthful explanations offered by the supposed criminal. He was the foreman of a mining company whose duty it was to oversee several mining operations. He was allowed a certain quantity of petrol to carry out his professional duties. If he siphoned off a bit for his own needs, this was a trivial matter in my opinion. But the filthy Boches, their minds distorted by vile propaganda, saw only the immediate reality: the motorbike, the petrol, Sunday. The conclusion was rapid: he was a partisan, an opportunist, a terrorist, and as such, not fit to be considered human. Once they had arrested him, they beat him up. When he arrived at the same place where I was being closely watched, his head was covered with a dressing, his face was bleeding. This bandage wasn't due to German kindness, needless to say.

The other suspect had been arrested at a friend's house in the countryside where he had spent the night. But he was carrying over 100,000 francs. His explanations, though very clearly stated, were regarded by the learned Germans as pure fantasy. Yet his arguments seemed conclusive. He was a horse-dealer on a business trip and only the night and the prospect of fun and a hearty dinner had made him break his journey. Indeed, his story was corroborated by the fact of the livestock show being held in the neighbouring town. But again, only the sum of money sparked their neurotic imagination. This too was suspicious.

Once the short interrogation was over, the presumed Resistance fighters who had been singled out were led away. We were extremely worried about this because we realised that they were heading towards new tortures and we were only reassured when they returned a few hours later. Even so, they came back in a sad state. The weakest had been beaten then tortured. The others, who looked much stronger, had been hit less violently, but had been subjected to a particularly depressing experience. Faced with their denials, the Nazi tormentors had tried the ultimate test: holding a gun against their temple, demanding a confession. Silence was the only response. Furious yet powerless, and not allowed to kill their victim because others after them would be trying out different tortures, they punched and kicked the steadfast refuser and finally let him go back.

When we heard about these crimes, we felt our own fists tightening but in vain, alas. Our powerlessness was stark. The machine gun stood out grimly on its mount and seemed to mock us with its crushing superiority. Our morning was thus rather painful. The Red Cross arrived somewhat late and we were fed in a mediocre fashion. In the afternoon, we had a pleasant surprise. Certain families who had been informed of our location had come to see how things were going with one of their own. Also, we were allowed to write letters, a great favour despite everything. Then parcels of hastily prepared food arrived to supplement our inadequate supplies. Still, few that day had the pleasure of writing to their loved ones or the benefit of a food parcel. But hope flickered in each person and we wished for some reconciliation the next day. And so, our day passed, tarnished in the morning by our first contact with the German, such as he is, and slightly cheered by the thought of exchanging letters with those we loved.

•

Night-time, the third night, was by and large more restful for each of us. We were getting used to our mean beds which made them seem less uncomfortable. The wall opposite began to look as if it had been designed for its current use and each man now went to relieve himself without any shame, while still skipping about to try to find a less soiled spot. And each man slept hoping for a sunny day.

This fourth day pleased just about everyone and at least we all took some pleasure from eating a lot and finally drinking a little wine. Those who had been left out were the guests of those who were better provided for. I also had the pleasure of reading a few anxiously written lines from my wife. She betrayed her fear at seeing me in this position in the few words that reached me. I consoled her as best I could and urged her to share my optimism. This situation couldn't go on. There had to be a solution soon. And this solution could only be our release, albeit without any apologies. This seemed to be the generally shared point of view on the third day of our imprisonment. We still weren't sufficiently demoralised to picture our future destiny. This was not least because the Nazi sympathisers among us could not in all honesty believe there would be a tragic outcome to this affair. They were even less aware than me of the greed, savagery and treachery of the wolves.

I mentioned the greed. I'll explain. The parcels that we received were opened beforehand and rifled through. The bread was cut into two, three or four pieces, the tins of food must have been energetically shaken about. These were certainly not unnecessary precautions; it was fair enough and in occupied territory, where rebellion could be glimpsed in every look, basic caution was essential. Supplies reached us all messed up. Impossible to tell with what special care and attention they had been prepared. We were also surprised, in the beginning at least, not to find any cigarettes or tobacco. And yet our brief correspondence had certainly emphasised this urgent need that we all felt. We soon found out from the replies that these requests had not been ignored. Our guards smoked continuously, and we soon realised the truth. This pathetic – even understandable – theft of an inessential thing was not the only one.

Other supplies were misappropriated. Those that made us think of how much our wives or our mothers cared. An entire stock of carefully hoarded chocolate was handed over for the poor absent one, a tin of concentrated milk that would improve the ersatz coffee, juicy preserves saved for the big occasions were lined up very carefully in readiness for the next shipment. Nothing but the best for us, it seemed. And so what became of these special treats? The filthy soldiers kept all these good things. They enjoyed them at our expense with no hint of shame. We got any left-over food that boorishly they didn't think was up to their standard. It was enough to delight us. It was the only good thing we had in this awful place under the watch of these morally deformed creatures.

On the fourth day, we were taken over to a trough in groups of ten or twelve where we sluiced ourselves down. This brief trip took place every day and we waited for it impatiently. We breathed more easily and the odours from the town, free despite the occupier, seemed to us quite invigorating. It is in this sad place, I think, that I ate the first cherries. The month of May was nearly over and in its turn was followed by all the charms of the burgeoning spring.

•

A few more days passed. Our optimism soon faded and the horizon darkened in our souls. The suspects had gone, taken to a large town to be interrogated more 'scientifically'. Those of us left behind no longer hoped for our freedom. We guessed our fate. Germany was waiting for its livestock; its own workforce, many of whom were mobilised on various fronts, was not sufficient for the industries of war. The neighbouring livestock, already subjugated for a long time, was probably not enough. Working the land demanded strong backs. That's what many of us thought; others, more perceptive, said there were more than enough workers in Germany and that we couldn't be of any use in this respect. The camp was waiting for us, along with inactivity and hunger. And yet no one suspected that for many this journey itself would signal their end. Personally, I predicted part of the truth but I couldn't discern just how far Nazi barbarity could go in both morally and physically annihilating a human being.

The different possibilities of our departure became clearer by the day. We were assured that our future destination was still on French territory. That comforted us a bit, but doubts persisted. We were beginning to glimpse the German mentality.

Soon we got to the morning of the tenth day; all of our happy carefree feelings of the first few hours had given way to an indefinable bitterness. At every moment, we were expecting bad news. On that day, the light was luminous. Through the smeared panes of the windows we could glimpse blue sky, so wide and blue. To crown the month of May, on this last day the sun was sending out warmer rays that caressed our skin. The town had never seemed so gay, so full of laughter. Nature seemed suddenly to blossom in all its grace, all its languid beauty. It bathed us in maternal concern, called us to life, to joy, to love.

FIVE

THE WAITING ENDS

Roland had always been someone agile enough to escape an unpleasant or tricky situation, a bit of a ducker and diver. Recounting his early youth before the intervention of military service and the descent into war and general disintegration, it is clear he had been used to fending for himself.

When he was about five or six years old, Roland was put into private boarding school in Livry-Gargan, a suburb of Paris, along with his sister who was two years older.

•

FROM ROLAND'S MEMOIR
The headmistress was a wealthy, lively person who led the institution expertly. Her husband was puny and inconsistent and was just an assistant who took care of the material things. I think she was particularly attentive to me, almost maternal; she didn't have any children. My sister and I had to stay as boarders for at least two years, i.e. the length of a colonial tour (two years followed by six months' leave).

Thus, we spent each leave period with our parents and lived a family life. These travels every two years led us to Dijon, among other places, where I remember my first experience of primary school. A single incident stays with me. As a newcomer, I was of course subject to teasing and other annoying things, even if quite mild, during the break. But at going-home time, more serious threats and gibes meant that I had to run away. For my own defence, I sought out the protection of a passing adult by running around him, which made the mob keep away. This adult took me under his wing and the hunters scattered.

Then the following period was a time of continuity. In Dijon my parents finally took care of my future schooling and contacted the classical grammar school (Lycée Carnot) and the professional lycée. The latter was able to take me because I didn't have the primary school certificate. I never took the exam because I was never properly prepared. So I went into Year 7 (*sixième B* I think, which didn't teach Latin or Greek). I don't remember anything about these first years. Of course I repeated Year 7 and did Year 8 more or less badly. Even so, despite my mediocre school attainment, my athletic qualities and my extraordinary liking for all team sports made me into a local star. I shone in all my favourite sports – basketball, football, athletics – and if I only gained one prize by the end of the school year, it was in PE.

I don't know what possessed me, demon or angel, but in Year 10 (*troisième*) I signed up to the scholarship exam, without any hope of succeeding. Then, surprise, I was accepted, which allowed me to join Year 11 (*classe de seconde*) without a prior probationary exam. It was still relatively calm on the international front at this time, but I suppose for the sake of the three children's schooling my mum moved permanently to Villeneuve-sur-Lot in France, and of course, my dad continued with his professional career in West Africa.

So I became a day pupil at the high school (Vieux Collège), my sister went to the girls' school and my younger brother attended one of the primary schools in town. I have specific memories of this time. My schooling was pretty much similar to my Dijon experience. Mediocre results always and moving on to the higher class by the skin of my teeth. I was made to stand in the corner after my first French composition by the Head of School, called the Principal at that time.

The person who was announcing the results came to my mark and position (last I suppose) and launched into a veritable diatribe about me. How on earth did I win the scholarship exam when the current result was the sign of an incomprehensible ignorance for a Year 11 student. I was stoical, took it in my stride without flinching and even without any bitterness. I was vaccinated against my scholarly mediocrity because I could always refer to other criteria, intellectually deficient perhaps but at a high level physically, yesterday, today and tomorrow.

And so, despite these excessively severe admonitions, I passed through Year 11 relatively satisfactorily. It was no longer about being mediocre, but about the just passable. It's true that this high school was privileged. The classes were small, on average ten to fifteen students per section, and I had to make an effort to keep myself in the last third, come good or bad year. The crucial Bac exam came along quickly. And I would have had to put in the effort throughout the year, but making light of my good intentions, my main preoccupations were sport: Thursdays in school, Sundays with the local team, the adult team and in the French championship league.

The written exam was a toss-up. This kind of cramming had worked well for me before the Bac.

However, in the last month I got down to studying the curriculum seriously but, with only limited time, I had to cram.

(My particular) D-Day arrived. I did what I could, always in the same relaxed way; I did my best, and by the end I had no idea what the result would be so I didn't worry about it. The next day a friend came to tell me that I was accepted. Off we went to the neighbouring village to buy the newspaper and confirm this good but unexpected news. The written exam was done, but the hardest part still had to be done, because if I had crammed for this first test, I had completely neglected the oral. Two subjects, history and geography, were not included in the written exam. These two subjects were my nemesis. My memory of this is very clear. I crammed for the essays on these subjects too, but not that much. The results were conclusive: all good or all bad, and bizarrely these results alternated. It was the same thing too for the oral exams during the year – this scoundrel of a Roland always managed to catch up from one exam to the other. To such an extent that the teacher always gave the same judgement: 'Chopard, you've redeemed yourself.' But the moral of the story is that the mark that the teacher put in my school report was terse and unimaginative: a diagonal line.

At the end of this route to the Bac it was the oral that was fatal for me. Confronted by the examiner, I babbled lamentably in answer to the questions and a vague smirk of disappointment crossed my face that the teacher might have interpreted as a sign of indifference, even of scorn.

Having failed, I spent my holidays in the countryside. I spent about a fortnight taking it easy (always my relaxation, mixed with being carefree) and did a bike tour with two friends. We went along the Atlantic coast from Bordeaux to Hendaye and back, and I started my revision on the two subjects, carrying it out conscientiously and assiduously. The moment of the oral arrived and I had no fears about my weak points as I had worked really hard. When I saw my examiner I had a vague premonition. It was the same one who had failed me in July and this bastard, I'm certain of it, marked me down even though my answers to the questions were correct.

Ultimately, my studies were rewarded with a pass mark, the lowest mark possible.

But I was twenty years old and what was I to do? I had to complete military service: do it now or ask for a deferment so I could get on with my studies. Given the digressions, the folly, the incoherence of my past academic life, I chose to do my military service. And so, I knowingly threw myself into two years of complete physical and mental deprivation. I lost two years of my youth without any compensation. Sport had been what motivated me but I couldn't do it anymore. And then came the war and complete degeneration.

•

Annie says the family often joked about Roland going to a *camp de vacances,* a Butlins, in Germany.

'*Non, non, non, je ne veux pas, je ne veux pas,*' ('No, no, no, I don't want to, I don't want to') he would reply. The children didn't question this too deeply. It was just Papa being his funny self. Now, however, having unearthed the memoir, having read about his experiences, now they understand.

From September 1943 through the summer of 1944, the Germans carried out a systematic deportation of members of the Resistance and of Jews, whether in the Resistance or not, while at the same time increasing the terror and violence against all civilians. The pace of deportations escalated in 1944.[32] In the days leading up to Roland's capture, there were mass deportations of maquis from a variety of locations. Camps were filling up. On 20 May, 1,200 Jews were deported to Auschwitz. On 21 May, while Lacapelle-Biron was enduring its own fearful misery, another 2,000 men already under arrest were taken from Compiègne to the Neuengamme concentration camp, near Hamburg – the first such large convoy of Resistance members to be sent there.[33]

Once Roland had been taken prisoner, he had no idea what would happen next. Ten days later, he found out.

•

FROM ROLAND'S MEMOIR

Divine daylight, evil day! On that day, in fact at around 14:00 hours, we were given the order to pack our bags. It was a simple enough task to gather up our rags, carefully clutch a few rare relics, bundle up the last supplies. There was an inspection two hours later. We were not supposed to be equipped with any knives or sharp objects. They seized the few pocket knives that people carried with them as a precaution and which had not been found during the first searches. The offenders weren't even punished. Our Krauts believed the circumstances were already tragic enough without aggravating them, which would have been quite pointless anyway. No physical suffering could be any worse than our mental suffering.

In columns, three at a time, each man carrying a bundle lopsidedly either on the shoulder or under an arm, our band moved off. Outside our dormitory, another delay. The Krauts, armed to the teeth, holding their guns, sweating and panting oafs, surrounded us in great numbers. Once each of them had got into their place on either side of our long column, the order to move out was given. We crossed several small courtyards in the neighbourhood, then the main courtyard, which you can easily picture because it looked like every other courtyard in the neighbourhood. The

....
32   https://www.sciencespo.fr/mass-violence-war-massacre-resistance/en/document/chronology-repression-and-persecution-occupied-france-1940-44.html
33   As above.

great iron gate was wide open and we tramped down the avenue. Outside, some of us saw our loved ones for a last time. My wife and my mother were there. I was the last one in the column so they thought for a moment, for a brief instant, that I wasn't part of this bleak convoy. But all of a sudden, they caught sight of me. Their grief weighed on me more than my own sorrow. Weeping, they gave me their final pieces of advice. I reassured them as best I could, uttered words of hope, but in vain; whether I liked it or not, my general appearance, my unusually pale face despite the warm air, clearly reflected my state of mind. A large bundle balanced unsteadily on my shoulder completed the miserable picture.

In spite of everything, my spirits were good. My mother and my wife followed me at a distance up to the train platform, because the passenger station had been closed in these circumstances, in a last nod to decency after exposure to a civilised country. Cattle cars were waiting for us.

On the platform, the Red Cross made its last and copious distribution of supplies. The journey would be long and boarding started – 50 men per carriage. Despite the debilitating spectacle, our heartbroken families wanted to seize every moment right up to the last minute to gaze on the faces of their loved ones. Then the sliding doors, creaking and grinding, closed on their cargo and shut us in the shadows. A last blown kiss, then darkness.

An era had passed. A blessed era during which lightness of being, confidence, freedom from worry, laughter, love, kindness sometimes, charity always – all of these had reigned. A peaceful, pacifist generation, given to good as well as to bad, but the latter always confined within given limits. In spite of the defects inherent in every people, we could feel proud of a certain degree of civilisation. We distinguished ourselves from the beasts through a clear idea of good and evil. In depressing times, we knew how to master our feelings; when it was necessary, we knew how to repress our instincts. In short, we had respect for human dignity both for ourselves and for others.

Once imprisoned, we sat down on our bundles. The railcar was quite narrow and there wasn't space for everyone to find a decent spot. Legs had to intertwine, backs were against backs. For better or worse, somehow we managed to settle down. The darkness seemed less dense. Soon the heat from outside and our animal heat combined to make the atmosphere extremely hot. Even though the march had been slow, our sweat became more profuse. We sought out slits or holes to breathe in a bit of outside air, which seemed fresh to us.

I stood up, I looked around our new prison and saw, not without some astonishment because I knew how careful the Krauts were, that the bolts in the ceiling were unscrewed. The boards barely resisted when you pushed them. I understood immediately what the railwaymen had done. Knowing what use these cars were put to, they thought to anticipate our intentions and to help us carry them out. I was grateful to them. I shared this discovery and its significance with my comrades. I assured them that escape was possible, easy even. Unfortunately, my suggestion did not get the reception it deserved. The Krauts' threat to shoot ten hostages on the spot if there was an escape attempt had snuffed out any idea of rebellion in most of them. I tried to explain how this threat was all part of war but that it wouldn't be carried out if the case arose. In vain, as this group of country people, terrified and short-sighted, hoped they would still serve as industrial or agricultural livestock. In spite of the informative spectacle of the last few days, they believed that the regime of beatings would stop and that they would be allocated a job that took their skills into account. And finally, food, even if not fine, at least enough of it, would ensure that the good will and application of these workers would be rewarded. Even a single escape attempt would be impossible, especially in the face of opposition by one's own fellow citizens. Fear would have made more than one of them commit the unforgiveable cowardly act of calling out for help from our hated enemies.

With a shrill whistle, the wheezing response of the engine, slowly and laboriously the convoy moved off. We were surprised at the direction we were going in. In fact, we were heading towards a rugged, wooded area where many Resistance groups had set up their bases. The train gradually picked up some speed and we rolled through the countryside. The journey was short. The train was slowing down gradually, indicating that we would stop soon and we did, in fact, stop about 30km from our point of departure. 'Now what?' we were all thinking. The scene spread out around the station was telling enough, although we could only glimpse snatches of it. Lorries loaded with civilians and predominantly with inmates of a nearby prison drove up at regular intervals and discharged their human cargo next to the station. Here a surveillance team, or should I say a deployment of troops, oversaw the organisation and counting of the new arrivals. Boarding took place when the prison had been emptied of all its occupants and we were all assembled on the platform.

Our doors were open. Each railcar had an equal distribution of men. With around ten companions, we got into a carriage already holding about 20 prisoners. They were dressed in prison uniform, all with shaven heads and wan faces, and had a sinister look. Two of them were stretched out along one of the sides. They had been literally butchered by their vile guards. Their faces bleeding, their breathing laboured, their eyes devoid of expression, they seemed to be dying. Once the doors were closed, their comrades told us the story of their evacuation. We knew that this prison, known as a colony, was mainly reserved for political prisoners and members of the Resistance. There was also a small number of ordinary convicted criminals. The group therefore made up a caste especially hated by the Boches. They wanted to make sure they didn't escape and had decided on their expatriation…

Their transportation to the station was particularly dramatic. The moment they emerged from their dismal incarceration, their hands on their heads, they were beaten violently. Each time they climbed into or got out of a vehicle, they were kicked or hit with a rifle butt. Others made the journey to the station on foot, closely guarded – a distance of about 15km. On this long march, the Germans could satisfy their primitive instincts. They struck the men for no reason. Reaching the station was seen as a relief. A few more blows and they would finally be in the railcars, uncomfortable but sheltered from an incredible and pointless brutality. Our fate already seemed more privileged than theirs.

The two unfortunate wounded men were not tended to at all. We couldn't help them in any way. No linen, no water. They were put in a ventilated spot where they could breathe more easily. We were also lucky to be in a carriage that was particularly well adapted. There were secure grilles installed low down on each side wall at the height of the troughs and the wagon was also equipped with regular vents. As a result, the car was well ventilated and we had a reasonable view of the places we were travelling through. This time we assumed that we wouldn't be getting out again until the end of the journey so we settled ourselves down as well as we could. Each of us had enough space to sit down or to stretch out, and the most significant thing was being able to breathe freely.

Our companions had received a package of food supplies from the Red Cross. Once the prisoners were settled and had recovered their breath and their spirits, they greedily ate some of the treats that they had been deprived of for so long. Gingerbread and fruit jellies seemed to them to be a fine dessert, then came the cheese, a sort of creamy gruyère, which they polished off with gusto; we gave them a bit of bread and also a little water from our meagre supply, a few litres if I remember correctly, which they found delicious. Watching this impromptu feast whetted our appetites and we dined, squatting in front of an improvised paper tablecloth.

Meantime, the door of our accommodation had been locked. Boarding operations were all complete. The convoy once again moved off. This time we went in the opposite direction from the first one. Stunned yet again by events, we stayed seated, still, deep in thought – or so it appeared at least. Suddenly, we heard a violent explosion. It seemed to have taken place beneath our own railcar. The train slowed down and stopped. Our guards got down and presumably went to find out the cause of this blast. Rapid steps on the stone ballast indicated febrile, noisy activity. It was dusk; the perfect time for an attack. Our captors themselves must also have felt a certain fear. Yet nothing unusual occurred. Slowly the excitement outside died down. The shouts, the hoarsely issued orders became less frequent. We expected our interrupted journey to begin again quite soon. A fellow from Alsace could understand some of what was being discussed outside and some of the specific details were enough to let us guess at the origins, the cause and the aim of this explosion.

The maquis (the clandestine local cell of the Resistance) had hastily put a banger on the rail track. This was supposed to blow up when the train ran over it, cause a split in the rail and derail the train. A more effective night-time operation was probably supposed to save us or at least aid our escape. Unfortunately, in their haste or rather because of their inexperience, our bombers misplaced the explosive device. It only blew up towards the end of the convoy and without severing the rail cleanly. The last few wagons continued on their way and this first attempt failed. Our journey proceeded. Darkness had taken over our lodgings. This particularly tough day, both mentally and physically, especially for our comrades, had worn us out. It didn't take long for us to fall asleep.

Our sleep was partly disturbed when the train slowed down or made a very brief stop. But if a stop went on for a while, our curiosity woke us up completely, especially because we wanted to follow exactly the chosen route. One stop went on for some time so we were able to wait for sunrise and cheer ourselves up a bit watching the bustling scenes in a large station. In fact, we were at Bordeaux, standing at the entrance to the concourse, right in the middle of the station.

At dawn, our dogs came to open the doors, brandishing their weapons. We climbed down two by two and got some relief under the wagons. We were able to get our bottles filled with water thanks to some obliging railway workers and to the unexpected laxness of our guards. The Krauts understood how important the water was and also were well aware that soon thirst would kill us, so I don't ascribe this favour to a transitory kindness but more to their sadistic love of contradictions.

In this town of Bordeaux, I even had the chance to taste a well-known red wine which was nectar to me. Did I foresee prolonged deprivation? This last bottle was brought to one of our companions by one of his friends. The Krauts paid no attention to an ordinary-sized bottle, ignorant of the finer points of this wine. A litre of any old wine would have been more to their liking. That's why we could enjoy it one last time. Unfortunately, this long stop was finally over. And we carried on. Our ample supplies meant we could eat plenty. The water was sufficient to quench our thirst even though it was bland compared to the wine.

Wherever we stopped at different stations, our visit aroused interest. These railcars with their cargo of closely watched men with grimy pallid faces, wide-open quizzical eyes, most of them dressed in homespun prison uniforms and wearing self-explanatory caps, left a false impression. At first glance, in fact, we looked like bad lads, a rough lot you wouldn't want to meet in a dark alley. A few words were enough to make people understand where we came from and their indifference or instinctive recoiling gave way to great compassion.

We made two or three stops a day in order to see to our bodily functions. These usually took place at marshalling yards or out in the countryside. We had already been going for two days. We reached Meaux station where we stayed for several hours. We were near the freight yard. Our pedantic masters had the good idea, a pretty rare one for them, of having us breathe

the fresh air. The doors were opened and we were able to breathe in freely lungfuls of an air that, on this particular day, was purer and fresher than any I had ever known. Then the station staff, and many others I think, abandoned their professional duties in order to make sure we were supplied with water. Each railcar received several pails of water that already seemed delicious to us and each one of us could drink our fill, which for a strong thirsty man is very satisfying, giving an inexpressible sense of well-being, a renewal of one's soul, you could say.

After having received this tonic which restored me and made me forget my situation, I came back to reality. The location lent itself to an escape, even an individual one. Unfortunately, I didn't try it. Should the opportunity arise again, I would not hesitate to defy the 50/50 chance I would have of being killed. In fact, all of us working together as one could have risked it on this liberating adventure. The prospect of success then would have been at least 90 per cent. Ten metres to run, a leap onto the loading platform and there, right there, your life would be saved for sure. The platform, crowded as it was with barrels, bales, crates, would have protected us from bullets and made our escape easier. Sadly for some of our comrades who died over there, there was no attempt at escape, deliverance was scorned.

If memory serves correctly, this second stop was the last where we were able to breathe the fresh air of freedom almost within our reach and see compassionate and smiling civilians practically among us, living freely without too many restrictions.

On the third day we reached Compiègne – the main camp for assembly and departure. Our arrival provoked a second deployment of Nazi strength. Once we were reorganised along military lines, an arrogant and overbearing officer in boots armed with a riding whip, acting as if he were the conqueror and invincible, gave us advice or rather the usual threats. Any attempt at escape was pointless, his weapon – and he patted his sub-machine gun – did not often miss, a hail of bullets would stop our flight. The last stage of our journey had lowered our spirits so much that the thought of another attempt barely even entered our heads. Pathetic twentieth-century German psychology. What has become of your *'Kultur'*? What will remain of this Nazi epic? Nothing but blood, blood, blood.

•

COMPIÈGNE

This name, this place, is thick with significance.

The Armistice of 11 November 1918, which came into force at 11 in the morning Paris time, marked the ending of the First World War and the surrender of Germany. Fighting on the Western Front stopped. There would still, however, be further steps to take before the signing of the Treaty of Versailles on 28 June 1919 which officially signalled peace between all the European nations.

The Armistice was signed in a railway carriage in the Rethondes Clearing in the forest of Compiègne. This place Compiègne signified shame, *die Schande*, for Germany. Twenty-two years later, while the town of Compiègne was being firebombed by the German army, in this same railway carriage General Huntziger, fighting back tears, was signing the Armistice of 22 June 1940 containing the terms of the French surrender to Germany.[34] (Shirer, p. 538.)

Before getting into his Mercedes *blindée* (tank), Hitler commanded that the copper rails of the railway carriage should be sawn up and the pieces distributed as souvenirs to the soldiers on duty for the Armistice signing in the forest clearing. He also ordered that the carriage itself and other monuments should be sent immediately to Berlin.

The choice of Compiègne as the main railway station and assembly point for the mass deportations was part of this psychological game-playing by the occupiers.[35] (Bernadac, p. 20.)

The French military base of Royallieu lies to the south of Compiègne. Compiègne-Royallieu, known as Frontstalag 122, was one of the biggest Nazi transit and internment camps in occupied France, in use between June 1941 and August 1944. More than 45,000 people passed through the camp, mainly political prisoners and *résistants*, on their way east to concentration and extermination camps. Within Royallieu stood 'Camp C', or the 'Jewish camp'. This part of Royallieu was an extermination camp in itself. The Jewish prisoners were starved to death.

....
34 William L. Shirer (1984). *The Nightmare Years 1930–1940, Volume 2*. Boston: Little, Brown & Co.
35 Christian Bernadac (1970). *Dachau ou le Train de la Mort*. Paris: Éditions France-Empire

FROM ROLAND'S MEMOIR

We made our way through the town. The inhabitants couldn't hide their emotion at this tragic sight, even though they were used to such convoys. Our apparently endless column must have been pitiful. Some people, women in particular, were even unable to contain their rancour and hatred for the vile occupiers and called out words of contempt. This sympathy for us, this shared feeling against the oppressor, was a fleeting balm for our pain.

We reached the camp after having passed through several barriers reinforced with bunkers. The camp, built according to the German method with the entrance flanked by two high watchtowers on pilings, looked grim from the outside. We entered, crossed a big yard that was completely empty, and were led to a small yard via a narrow path lined with barbed wire. After waiting for an hour, the usual roll call took place and we were led to our new dwellings in groups of varying sizes. This camp was a huge barracks and we found ourselves on familiar territory. It was there that the first stage of our life as deportees began.

All the policing and the internal bureaucracy of the camp was in the hands of the French. In a friendly way they brought us up to date on our new duties. This was a little like life on an army base, although within strict limits, whose adjutant this time demanded outward signs of respect, of submission. He was a Kraut and we had to take off our caps each time we crossed his path, a hundred times if necessary. We were advised in general to salute anything that was Jerry or appeared to be Jerry, even the dog. Each morning and evening there was a general roll call. All the detainees, organised by building, were counted. This roll call only lasted at most half an hour.

At Compiègne we became familiar with hunger. Our supplies had run out during the journey. I think it was on the second day at the camp that we received a 5kg package from the Red Cross, plain biscuits, fruit jellies, jam, sugar. It meant we could satisfy our hunger for a few more days. Then suddenly, a new diet that seemed to us to be worse than what we had had up to then, which had satisfied our appetites. The routine of soup twice weekly was established by the Red Cross. It was distinguished by the presence of meat and abundant vegetables, but even so it wasn't enough to restore balance to our menu. This was a particularly painful period.

An intelligently and extensively stocked library was a precious relief for us and I used to read a book each day. We preferred to spend time in a shady spot in the big yard. But we were continually and fiercely plagued by hunger pangs. Those who had a little money were able to improve their daily diet at a canteen. The 10 or so francs that I had managed to keep hidden from the various investigations at the beginning, almost without my realising it, were just enough to pay the borrowing charges for the books. Some of the others played football. I was passionate about team sports and used to play football right from my early boyhood, so I couldn't resist the temptation and joined in.

Playing carefully, limiting my activity, I was soon forced to notice an unexpected breathlessness and an exhaustion never felt before. So I stopped playing. The next day I was worn out and it took several days before I was back to normal. Those who could indulge in sustained physical effort without any ill effects were the favoured ones, the skivers in this camp. Here too, unfortunately, the social hierarchy asserted itself. A slightly forced comparison might push me to say that a feeble minority represented the nobility and the rest, the poor starving masses, the proletariat. Wealth was measured not in gold, diamonds, land, castles, but in physical appearance.

For example, some genuine old marquis, charged with sharing out the Red Cross parcels, was promoted to duke or count by virtue of his new post. Some other man, son of a colonel or even of a general, couldn't be anything less than a policeman. Also, there were many middle-class men among the oppressed, belonging to every layer of that class. What is more, they adapted stoically to their new plight and soon became integrated into the mass of unfortunates. Our ruling class had their servants. They accepted this horrible drudgery because it was well rewarded. They profited from the plentiful leftovers from the daily feasts of their masters. Relations were cordial between us, their orders were imbued with friendship, but that didn't mean I blamed their outrageous selfishness any less.

Outrageous, yes, because the Red Cross supplies piled up in their bedrooms were going off. The bread was getting mouldy. And their daily rations of perishable goods, butter for example, were supplemented at the expense of ours. I am confirming these facts openly because they were told to me by a 'servant'. And I still see this old marquis over and over again – was he really a marquis? – always well turned out, properly shaved, properly dressed, his face beaming, the nose slightly swollen and ruddy from alcohol, who supported unwaveringly and with good reason a regime under which youth was withering away.

In the evening, when night fell, we were obliged to stay inside the buildings. Whoever disobeyed could be shot dead. When a convoy arrived, and many others followed ours, a shrill whistle ordered the immediate return to our rooms.

SIX

THE NORMANDY LANDINGS, D-DAY 6 JUNE 1944

Remnants of the Normandy campaign are everywhere in the part of France where my family has a house. It is located on the Cotentin Peninsula, about 7km from Utah Beach, where the American troops landed on D-Day, or *Jour-J* in French. You can't avoid the remains of bunkers, batteries and lookout posts along the great, bare beaches of the peninsula. In nearby Sainte-Mère-Église, one of the first towns to be liberated on D-Day, the whole local economy thrives on Second World War memorabilia and commemorative events. The town is particularly famous for the story of one of the paratroopers from the US 82nd Airborne Division, John Steele, who landed on the side of the church tower, and was trapped there hanging from his parachute while fighting raged beneath him. He survived, and the town continues to display a model of John Steele in his parachute, hanging from the church tower. (This scene is memorably recreated in an American epic film about the invasion, *The Longest Day*.[36])

In the months and weeks leading up to 6 June, the town takes on again the febrile air of that time. Men and women, their children, of many nationalities, meet up to take part in the events – dressed up in military uniforms or the fashions of the era, some driving around in authentic

---

36 *The Longest Day* (1962). Based on the book *The Longest Day* by Cornelius Ryan. Producer: Darryl F Zanuck Productions Inc. Distributor: 20th Century Fox.

American jeeps playing at being the liberators. Women in tight-waisted dresses from the 1940s, with red lipstick and hair tortured into stiff waves, belt out tunes of the time to appreciative audiences.

It is a strange experience to be part of, not nostalgic for this is not my history, but not completely unfamiliar. My very young mother was sent to work in a munitions factory for a brief period, until she was sacked for breaking too many parts and went off to become a driver, much more to her seventeen-year-old taste. My even younger father, an apprentice engineer who dreamed of driving a tank (a memory he would smile wryly about much later on in his life), was drafted into helping with the building of Spitfires.

Above our Normandy garden, large transport planes fly low overhead, sometimes carrying parachutists. From our skylight in the attic bedroom, we can watch the parachutes opening, the men drifting down to the now peaceful Normandy soil. One evening a few summers ago, we were sitting in the garden, with our glasses of wine, contentedly watching the show when we realised (quite slowly – we were several glasses down) that one parachutist had become detached from the rest and was floating down somewhere near our house… in fact, into the neighbouring field. We had to help. Glasses down, shoes on, we ran out of the gate, down the lane, reaching the road at the same time as other inhabitants of the hamlet. As if in a scene from *Close Encounters of the Third Kind*,[37] we found ourselves surrounded by people we had barely met before, all heading towards the same goal – the man in a parachute coming down towards us, needing our help.

He landed in a tree, hanging there, tangled and helpless. Our neighbour, with only one functioning arm, commanded his wife to fetch his chainsaw. He clambered up the tree, wedged himself in, beckoned for the chainsaw, and with the one functioning arm sawed off the branch that was trapping the airman. Others joined him in and around the tree and together they freed the man and his parachute. We onlookers stood around, watching excitedly.

It was thrilling and memorable. A glimpse into the past, however unreal.

•

---

37 *Close Encounters of the Third Kind* (1977). Written and directed by Steven Spielberg. Distributor: Columbia Pictures.

D-Day, codenamed Operation Overlord, was the start of the campaign to liberate Europe. It was the largest naval, land and air operation in the history of warfare. The landings did not mean an end to the war in Europe, but signified that victory was in sight.

Planning had already begun after the Dunkirk evacuation and in the years leading up to 6 June 1944, a huge force of soldiers was amassed in Britain. From December 1939, the Canadians started to assemble, then during 1943 and 1944, 1.4 million US servicemen arrived. My mother and my aunt both had American boyfriends, 'Johnny' and 'Mel'.

By 1944, there were over two million troops in Britain from twelve countries preparing for the invasion.

At 06:30h, Allied troops began landing on the five assault beaches; Utah, Omaha, Gold, Juno and Sword.

•

Roland welcomed the news of the invasion; he and so many others hoped that it signalled the eventual end of their imprisonment and their suffering. However, D-Day was only the beginning of the process, and Roland and his fellow slave labourers would have many months still to wait for the end. They had no idea of this, of course. Roland's initial optimism is poignant.

'Normandy was liberated, the Allied forces were launching themselves with all their strength towards the heart of France, and especially towards the west and southwest. Our hope was revived for a moment, then suddenly the order came for an unexpected roundup.'

When Roland wrote this, he knew the truth, he knew how much longer his imprisonment would last, but recollects that bitter moment of hope on that last day he would spend in French territory before his final release almost a year later.

The Battle for Normandy, the intense bombing and destruction of the stone farmhouses and hamlets in which the Germans had set up command centres, the general sacrifice of the land and the people to the greater aim of liberation, was protracted and difficult. Nor was it welcomed unequivocally by all the population. The wife of the Vichy mayor of Montebourg, the town nearest to my house, is quoted as saying the landings were the start of their misfortunes.[38] At least people had what they needed under occupation. Of course, not everyone shared these sentiments, but there were many who lived each day anxiously, fearful for their husbands, brothers, sons taken as forced labourers, caught in situations like Roland's, imprisoned in Germany, and for Resistance members arrested and sent to concentration camps.

The Normandy landscape is characterised by the *bocage*, where the lanes and roads lie between high hedgerows. This made it very difficult for Allied soldiers to penetrate in their tanks and easier for the Germans to defend. By the end of August 1944, more than three months since Roland's capture, the German army was in retreat from France, but by September, the Germans were able to regroup and launch a counter-offensive in the Ardennes in December 1944. It failed, but nevertheless slowed down the advance towards Germany and, ultimately, to liberation.

•

FROM ROLAND'S MEMOIR

A few pro-German newspapers arrived at our camp completely above board. So we found out the good news and especially the bad news. Dawn on 6th June found us at Compiègne. The next day, the newspapers reported on this victorious attempt at landing. 'The beachhead was narrow; the German forces weren't going to waste any time in mercilessly destroying this English pig-headedness.'

The reports were meaningless. Our faces beamed with pleasure. The long-awaited day was here. The horizon stretched brightly before us; our imprisonment was going to come to an end. I was elated. Our very hunger was overtaken by the intoxication of future promises. What talk, what furious hopes expressed. But the relentless passing of the hours continued unabated.

The beachhead had expanded, the Cotentin peninsula was in the hands of the invading liberator, Normandy was very close. Bitter fighting, the Germans' desperate but pointless resistance, did not deter the Allies' slow but sure advance. And yet at Compiègne our delirious optimism suffered some serious setbacks. A first convoy containing 1,100 men had left the town

---

38   Antony Beevor (2009). *D-Day: The Battle for Normandy*. London: Penguin Books.

for Germany. Our turn was imminent. The camp was overcrowded. Each morning, the coming dawn was greeted with terror. Up until eleven o'clock, we were on tenterhooks. Once past this hour, the bad news was put off until later, until the next day perhaps, and this next day was the focus of our fear.

The advance continued, the German front was broken. Normandy was liberated, the Allied forces were launching themselves with all their strength towards the heart of France, and especially towards the west and southwest. Our hope was revived for a moment, then suddenly the order came for an unexpected roundup. This time there was no doubt that a new convoy was to be formed. All my comrades from the original roundup were part of it, along with others, many others too. I will never forget this young blond Parisian, his hair in a crewcut, who right up until the announcement of this forced expatriation was full of outrageous optimism. Arguing that black was white, he made the case to us for the growing unlikelihood of a new evacuation. We listened to him open-mouthed, too happy to find a person with such a positive view, too keen also to believe him. He answered those who interrupted him or those who questioned him, eager for fuller details, with ever fresher arguments. Even he was part of the roundup.

I think that his plans were stopped right there. Did he come back? Did he die? His disappointment must have been huge, but I dare to hope that such optimism survived this heavy blow. Those destined for departure were collected together. We were told verbally the list of things to take and things to leave behind, under threat of punishment. Once this preparation for leaving was over, we were assembled and our kit and ourselves inspected in the afternoon at 15:00 hours. At 15:00 hours exactly, the whistle sounded, new roundup, new roll call, new group. There were 1,100 of us. In bands of twenty, fewer perhaps, we moved along in front of our masters. We were searched, holding our shoes, and our kit! I was able to conceal a pocketknife from their searches. I had slid it into my sock under my foot. I should point out that our stretching of the rules was not punished if we were found out.

Buildings carefully surrounded with barbed wire were our new lodgings. This time, no tiered wooden bunks to sleep on. To the right, to the left, straw. We had become mere livestock. We spread this straw out over the entire floor of the room and armed with our scarce and often negligible supplies we lay down.

Last nap on French soil. How many of us foresaw death approaching, how many of us guessed at future suffering, the next day's suffering? A movement of volunteers willing to plan an escape tried to meet up in one or two rooms. There was partial success (I was part of it). Skilfully constructed hacksaws concealed in some books had been even more skilfully stolen away from the rough and clumsy German searches. Hidden under belts, they escaped the notice of the bumpkins, the blockheads, the bastards, the oafs.

•

Then the next morning our departure was for real. Our first allocation was disrupted by the crush stupidly provoked by those who hung back the previous evening. Unfortunately, everyone suddenly wanted to react and to attempt the impossible. This meant the column which formed was a motley crew composed of an indiscriminate jumble of the pure and the impure, those who resisted from the beginning and those who had just joined (authentic Resistance fighters, against those who'd only been fighting since August or September). This last sentence will be understood by true Resistance fighters, of whom I was one, if not through my actions then at least in my heart.

Before we left the camp, they gave us each a round loaf of brown bread weighing about 1500gm and a sausage which, we were warned, was meant to last for three days. We thought this was a pleasant prospect. Then a march that was the opposite of the previous one took us to the station. There, we were broken up into groups of 100. And we got into cattle cars entirely German in origin. One, two, three, thirty, forty, seventy, yet more and more got in, we moved over a bit, eighty, ninety, we were getting squashed by now, ninety-two, ninety-three, ninety-four, finally the last one got in, but he was the hundredth. When the platform was emptied of its herd, an interpreter, pure Kraut, visited each cattle wagon.

New threats in case we tried to escape, then a friendly admonition recommending that we give up any sharp objects, knives etc. to our generous adviser. A cold welcome, the order was meant to be obeyed, a few frightened hands held out an inoffensive penknife. The order became a threat of serious punishment; some knives were brought out of some pockets. The threat became immediate execution, right there up against a wall. Those still left acquiesced, understanding their isolation and consequently, their powerlessness.

I cut a last bit of bread from my loaf that I'd already started and handed over the object of a completely unjustified desire. I had understood that yet again I was surrounded by sheep whose only ambition was to be led gently to the slaughterhouse.

The doors closed without any creaking this time. No one made any suggestion about trying to escape. Each man settled down as best he could for the final journey. About an hour's wait. The convoy moved off. The ordeal began. This time the partition walls were tightly sealed. Nowhere in the floor was light allowed to get in. The ceilings seemed to mock our impotence. Our only ventilation holes were two narrow openings diagonally across the side walls set at the height of a tall man – around 1m 75 or 80cms. A receptacle was placed in two of the corners which we easily guessed served as a toilet. Someone who still had a clear head, I don't know who, suggested that we should not stay standing up, that we shouldn't obstruct our two little skylights. The air could thus enter more freely.

The weather was grey when we got into the rail car and since then had darkened. Despite the season, darkness had filled our wagon by six in the evening. Pretty much everyone had eaten as much as they wanted; I was not worried about the next day so I had satisfied my hunger, eaten a third of my bread and half of my sausage; many others had saved their supplies. The night, the first one we spent as deportees, was painful. No one managed to find a position in which sleep was possible. Sometimes I grabbed some sleep, with my head on a leg, my body covered with other people's legs, my own legs on other people's bodies, but unfortunately it was all too brief. One of these jumbled-up legs, full of pins and needles under the weight, stretched out or folded up, so everything moved, there was grumbling, more lively complaints, and lovely welcome sleep disappeared, never to return. Small groups took it in turns quite randomly to stand up and straighten out a bit. The so-called 'windows' were hidden by thoughtless heads, shouts and remarks rightly brought the offenders back to the agreed-upon policy.

The following dawn did not surprise us at all. Our faces were haggard, our weariness was obvious. On the second day, the worst day of the journey, already few people ate. As for me, whose appetite knew no bounds, I made do with a bit of sausage and a piece of bread about the same thickness. The sun came out. We were still on French soil. But our destination was uncertain. We thought about letting our families know about our situation.

Each of us, not just the bravest, drafted a few words on a scrap of paper, or a few brief bits of news, or the equivalent of a letter. On a thin sheet of paper to the best of my ability I wrote about both the past and the probable future as a sort of historical document, which might – I suppose – have been my last communication with a beloved civilised world…

We gathered up our last thoughts, folded and refolded the paper to make it into a sufficiently heavy object, and as we were pulling out of a major train station, after attracting the railway workers' attention, we let fall our last goodbye.

•

THE LETTERS

Miraculously, those railway workers from the Société Nationale des Chemins de Fer Français (French National Railway Company) managed to collect up these folded and refolded bits of paper from where they had fallen onto the tracks and make sure they were forwarded to the appropriate place.

What follows is the letter Roland composed for Irène on that thin sheet of paper; even at that moment he was thinking of it as a potential historical document. Roland does not sound especially fearful nor despairing. He has no idea what awaits them.

•

ROLAND'S LETTER

Here we are on the eve of our departure for an unknown destination this time. And yet, we hope to stay in France. The stop at Compiègne was 'neutral' – the food was almost enough and we were able to sleep. My morale has been quite shaken by the news we're getting, whether true or not. I think that around Fumel it's quite quiet, that Christian [Roland's younger brother] went to Souliès. Our needs have been catered to partly by the Red Cross which has given each of us quite a well-stocked parcel. The sirens sound quite often but usually for nothing. My main pastime has been reading, there is quite a good library and we had a few successful social gatherings.

They gave us back our wallets, but of course they had removed any money and identity papers. I had a few photos but unfortunately not the one of Alex. I think he must be crawling by now.

Most of us are worried about the journey because of being uncomfortable or being in danger, but not me. It might offer us something unpredictable. No doubt we'll go back through Paris. All social classes are represented in our barracks – we've even got a few doctors.

I don't know if you will get this letter, but if you do, it's likely to be the only one. We aren't allowed letters and also I'm worried that they'll stop the post. *So please do not worry about me at all.* Our situation is not the worst one and there are at least 2,000 of us, so there's safety in numbers.

But you must make sure to comply with whatever rules are imposed on you. I send you all big hugs – and to Moncany, the grandparents and to everyone.

Big kisses.

•

Annie still has this letter, this thin piece of paper, folded and refolded. When she holds it, she feels as if her father's hand is reaching out through time to touch hers.

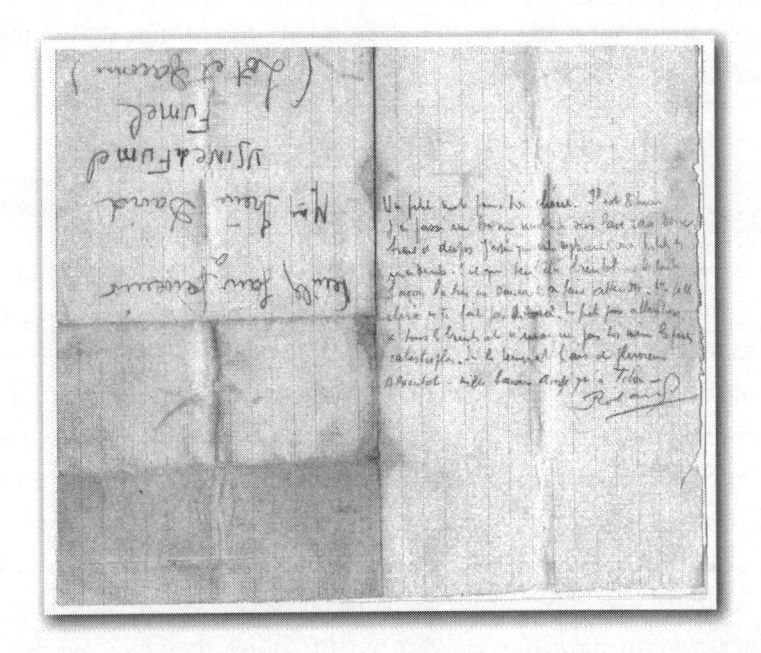

Front page of the letter that Roland folded and refolded and threw onto the railway tracks

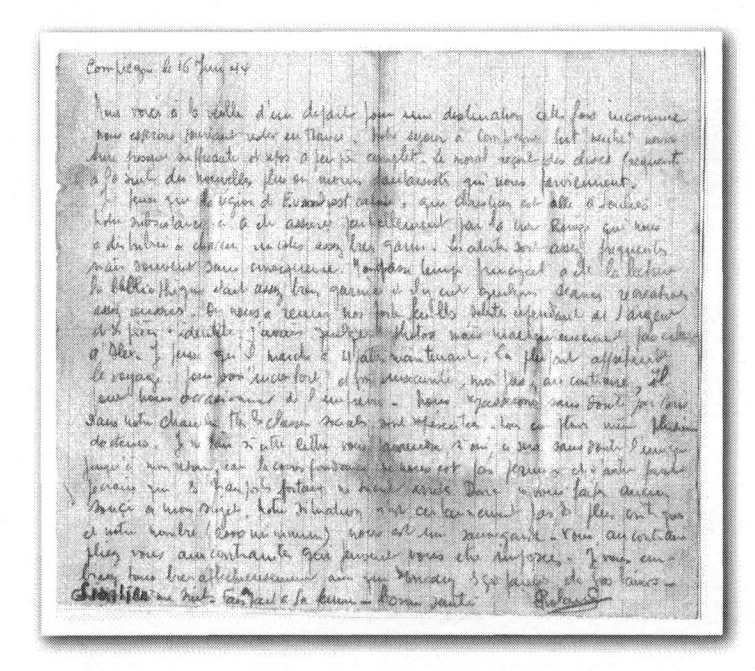

Reverse page of the letter

•

FROM ROLAND'S MEMOIR

The cloudy sky seemed to ooze bitterness. Its weight seemed to render the air motionless. The train seemed to slice through this intangible curtain with a mournful gasp. The air passed like an arrow in front of our skylights but did not enter. The atmosphere in the railcar had warmed up. Carbon dioxide gas levels had risen. Our breathing speeded up. Thirst started to torment us, exacerbated by the surrounding heat. Even the landscape was threatening. Often, we were rolling through deep valleys, bordered by rocky hills covered in fir trees where life must have been harsh, combative and fractious. We were obscurely aware of foreign soil.

It was nightfall. Each man dreaded this second night. It was just like the first only with dramatic scenes. Several of our companions were exhausted and starting to suffocate and were falling as they tried to reach the vent. Luckily, several strong, selfless men supported each fainting man and carried him to our window. The fresh night air, above all pure air, revived each of these poor men. There were only a few cases that night.

Thirst was tormenting us more and more. Large droplets of water were falling from the ceiling. We thought there was a gutter. These warm drops, dripping at intervals, were from our own breath. The nocturnal chill had cooled the sides of our railcars without unfortunately cooling down the interior. Of course, there was condensation. The night passed, the pale morning found us standing up, even more pale. The night's events had worn us out.

Each of us crouched down with great difficulty, our breathing apparently eased with the coming of the day, but nagging thirst was clinging to our lips, to our gullets. One canteen of water for more than twenty men was our only ration. Each one of us let a life-saving dribble spill onto our parched lips. The desire to seize this welcome flask with both hands, to guzzle it down, was difficult to control. We counted the ten seconds allocated to each one of us as fairly as possible. It went around three times. The small amount left over was kept for the probable fainters the next night. Discipline was respected in our carriage. Unfortunately, this wasn't the case generally. Some unruly men didn't know how to overcome their instincts. When they got the water, fights broke out and the strongest or meanest quenched their thirst, the weak ones or the fatalists got nothing, and some of the precious liquid was lost.

The approach to the window also presented the opportunity for some bizarre brawls. Exhausted, gasping men sacrificed their last strength, their last card, to a pointless, futile fight in which the two combatants soon went down. Their breathing, boosted by the effort, didn't have enough oxygen to sustain it. Soon they blacked out and nobody could help them reach the object of so much desire. Such things happened during the night. Two brothers could have killed each other without knowing it.

How many deaths could have been avoided if each man, aware of the danger, had forced himself to take only his share of water, if each man, aware of the importance of strict hygiene, had made do with just relieving his bladder, except in an emergency. If finally, and most importantly, our waste buckets had been emptied before being completely filled up. When they were full, they were too heavy and the contents could splash back into the wagon. Soon overflowing, they restricted our minimal space – not so crucial – but made the already unbreathable air stinking and tainted. Considering all of this, the men were splendid in the face of it all. The journey ended after seventy-five hours of travelling, seventy-five hours during which our door was only opened once.

At the Franco-German border, the guards were relieved and our contingent handed over. There was a headcount. Our door was wrenched open violently. We rushed out, frantic for clean air, only to back up immediately with the same haste. A Kraut, one foot on the first step, whip in his hand, was getting ready to climb up. He didn't want to rub shoulders with our mob. He was in a hurry mainly to carry out his task as quickly as possible. The tainted air, the foul stink, the stifling heat did not encourage a prolonged visit. A couple of swishes of the whip and we huddled fearfully in one half of the railcar.

The headcount began, sometimes some of the timid ones jumped over to the other side. This involuntary act of indiscipline, which provoked a mental effort by disturbing the rhythm of counting one by one, was punished with a violent crack of the whip. The last sick and ill ones were kicked and whipped into catching up with our group, dragging themselves painfully under the volley of swearing.

SEVEN
DACHAU

Dachau is one of those names, like Buchenwald, that is not simply the name of a place but a synonym for evil. This is where Roland was taken first.

Dachau was the first concentration camp, established by the Nazis in 1933, to incarcerate political prisoners. However, unlike prisons, the *Konzentrationslager* (KL) were not under any kind of judicial supervision. The prisoners did not go through any kind of trial nor were they convicted of any crime. The organisation of the Dachau camp became the model for the whole KL system as it grew.

Early camps were set up all over Germany, controlled by different groups and with different structures. Civilian authorities set up local detention centres to deal with people considered subversives who opposed the Nazi regime. They were imprisoned, intimidated, hidden. It was SS chief Heinrich Himmler's job to centralise the administration of the camp system, and from 1934 onwards, the SS took control, closing some camps, reorganising others along the lines of the original one at Dachau, and building huge new camps. In 1936, Sachsenhausen near Berlin made its debut, followed in 1937 by Buchenwald near Weimar, then Flossenburg outside Weiden, close to the Czech border, and Mauthausen, near the eponymous town in Austria. Ravensbrück camp for women, built in a swamp 80km north of Berlin, opened in 1939.

The early camps mainly detained German political prisoners, but as the system expanded, so did the intake of prisoners. Some were persecuted on religious grounds, others because they were 'asocials' or 'criminals' – homeless people and beggars, welfare recipients and casual workers, some homosexual men, gypsies, the disabled and sick, society's outsiders. (My mother-in-law, a German woman with epilepsy whose first husband died in the war, escaped incarceration and forced sterilisation. However, once the opportunity arose, she left Germany for the USA.) The Nazis were proponents of eugenics and in 1933, passed the Law for the Prevention of Offspring with Hereditary Diseases, designed to enforce the sterilisation of the disabled and chronically ill. Epilepsy was the third most common criterion used. Germany was not the only country to embrace eugenic beliefs.[39]

With the outbreak of the war, camps were used to incarcerate foreign prisoners from all over Europe. Then began the mass deportations of Jewish prisoners.

The KL system included twenty-seven main camps and spawned over a thousand subcamps during its twelve-year existence from 1933 to 1945.

•

DACHAU, NOVEMBER 2019

I went to Dachau by train on a day trip from Munich. The town is like any other – shops, hairdressers, bakeries, cafes, traffic. And on the day I went there, the skies were exceptionally lowering and grey. We had to wait for a special bus at the train station to take us to the concentration camp remains. The bus dropped us quite a distance from the camp itself and the walk there was quite circuitous, through side streets and along alleys lined with small industrial businesses, car parks and places that seemed to have very few people bustling about as you might expect. It felt quite a deserted place. And everywhere, pine trees towered.

We were rigorous in our explorations, reading all the information boards, trying to imagine ourselves arriving on a train, seeing the gates, the buildings, not knowing what lay ahead. Of course, it is impossible

....
39   https://www.wellcomecollection.org/articles/XkvmsREAACUAUWwN

to imagine such things. It is false and too dominated by the subsequent images we all have in our heads of what life must have been like. We must leave the descriptions to those who, like Roland, lived there, not knowing what would happen next. Each night he fell asleep with the lice and each morning he had no notion of whether that day might, in fact, be his last. But in any case, he wasn't thinking about the future. He was simply surviving from hour to hour.

Roland always considered himself a lucky man. He was able to come home.

•

FROM THE INTRODUCTION TO THE DACHAU CAMP:

'New concentration camps 1943–45: In 1943 the concentration camp system was again expanded. Some of the ghettos in the East were converted into regular concentration camps and put under the authority of the SS. The concentration camps Vaivara (Estonia), Riga (Latvia), Kauen (Lithuania), Lublin/Majdanek, Warsaw, Plaszow (Poland) and Herzogenbusch (Netherlands) were added to the already existing camps. A network of approximately 1,500 subcamps was created around these main camps. Most of the prisoners held in subcamps were forced to work for the armaments industry. In addition to providing slave labour, the concentration camps now served to intimidate the thousands of foreign forced labourers in the Reich. At the pinnacle of the "total war" in 1944, further concentration camps were established to fulfil new functions. Prisoners were mobilized in the Mittelbau-Dora concentration camp to construct a huge underground rocket factory. As of spring 1944, prisoners who were sick or unable to work were deported to the Bergen-Belsen concentration camp. They were given the barest provisions and left to die.'

•

Roland arrived at Dachau in early June 1944.

For Roland, Dachau was a relief, even if it was short-lived. The train journey was harrowing. Arriving at Dachau meant Roland and his fellow prisoners could at least get some fresh air.

FROM ROLAND'S MEMOIR

We welcomed our arrival at this station with relief. Our slow suffocation was coming to an end. The fresh air denied to us for more than three days was waiting for us there. A fourth night in this hellish railcar would have had unpredictable consequences perhaps, awful ones most certainly. The self-discipline we had exercised would have crumbled before the instinct for self-preservation. The gasping wild struggle, the true struggle for life itself, would have hastened the inevitable suffocation and the number of deaths would have been immense. *Dachau therefore seemed like a salvation.*

We understood very quickly once the doors had been opened that the German environment in all its aspects was hostile to us. We climbed down right in the middle of the train passengers. Our mournful convoy should have made every human being feel sorry for us. The five or six corpses, the hundreds of dying men being carried on stretchers and thrown haphazardly into a lorry, should have been enough to provoke, if not pity, then at least indifference. No, the civilians, men, women, children, all stared at us curiously, incapable of any feeling of compassion. They looked at some of us with a callous smile; our parched comrades hurled themselves into the puddles to drink the greyish, dirty, even putrid water. Not a compassionate glance, not a word of encouragement, not a gesture of pity. The children laughed, the young people sniggered, some women stared at us perhaps seeking to rediscover the physical attributes appreciated in former times. Our stubbled faces, our haggard eyes, our robotic gestures prompted nothing, nothing, nothing. Our procession regrouped, more pathetic than ever. The town watched us, uncaring, dully antagonistic, as we shuffled along hopelessly towards our destiny.

The camp was situated outside the town. We walked along a road that was badly maintained. The grass had pushed through. Hastily I bent down and grabbed a handful.

I chose it as best I could, tall and softly green. I chewed it to extract the sap. Even though the grass was bitter it moistened the mucous membranes of my mouth which I appreciated. The chewing process made me salivate and my thirst seemed less acute. We noticed some barrack buildings, most of them in ruins. A few detached houses seemed to have been cut down the middle. Groups of prisoners in uniforms striped lengthways in white and blue, white and green, white and blue-green were working to fill in giant cracks, restore a pathway, strengthen a bridge, repair pipes. It was cheap labour to which we would make a significant contribution.

This sight of burnt-out walls, of roofs torn off, of houses in fragments filled us with pleasure. For our part, this appalling devastation in other places, under other skies, seemed to us heaven-sent here, through anger perhaps, but primarily because of simmering hatred. We had indisputable evidence that our mental distress would be alleviated by the physical misery of the German people. From that day on I understood that the air-raid siren would always be a welcome sound for me, that the roar of the aeroplanes, the dreadful thunder of the blind bombings, which could kill me, would awake in me this need for hope, this thirst to find happiness once again.

The gateway appeared. Tall, broad iron gates, surmounted with a small square tower, dominating both the interior of the camp and its immediate exterior. On each side high electrified barbed wire fences surrounded the camp. Behind this wire fencing for a stretch of about 8 to 10 metres there was a forbidden zone, crammed with barbed wire, which would have been difficult and dangerous to get into. The notorious watchtowers, placed at regular intervals quite close together, stood guard constantly day and night with a vigilant and tireless eye. We went in.

Vast buildings, ancillary to the camp, lined a wide avenue. Then a huge, immense yard appeared, bare and greyish, the surface marked only by two goalposts. Soon the yard turned to a blackish colour. Our bodies were covering it. Each man collapsed onto his meagre bundle, not to sleep but finally to stretch out. An inexpressible relief seemed to carry us to the land of dreams as we spread our bodies out without embarrassment. We no longer even felt thirst; we were simply overwhelmed with fatigue. A bizarre sense of well-being overcame us. Several men fell asleep, but most were waiting for the crowning moment of their greater well-being, the flourishing of their peace of mind regained, after seventy-five nightmarish hours of confinement.

The roll call had begun. In groups of about forty we were moved towards the disinfecting and dressing room. Before that we were given a warm drink of tea, with sugar no less.

It isn't possible to express the depth of our delight as we drank this tea; I believe I may never again experience a comparable physical satisfaction. We were offered a second solace: a shower. We stripped off in an enormous hall. All our belongings were taken and put in a paper bag bearing our names and our registration numbers. Valuable items were also put into a little paper pouch. What care taken for our meagre material resources!

Finally naked, we went before a 'panel' charged with noting down our details, name, first name etc. Our questioners were deportees, mostly foreign, mainly Polish. They seemed to radiate health, even vigour, with their shaven heads and round faces. I later found out that they were priests and as such were subjected to a more favourable regimen. After our details had been taken, the warm shower gave us back a bit of strength. We had been sheared beforehand, every surface shaved. Then we were disinfected on the shaved parts with a paintbrush, which provoked a real burning sensation for a few minutes. I clenched my teeth stoically. The pain became less sharp and calmed down. Naked, laundered, without a hair on us, somewhat restored, we were unrecognisable.

We went into the clothing warehouse. Well-used civilian clothes stained with paint were distributed. Each man received a shirt, trousers, a jacket. Our shoes were made in a rudimentary fashion: wooden soles and fabric uppers. At the slightest acceleration in your step, the shoe fell off. When there were quite a few of us, a German, an inmate himself, took us to our bunkhouse, Number 19 I think, a long building divided into four units. I belonged to the fourth unit. I met up with a few comrades from whom I had been separated when we left Compiègne.

Others arrived later on. Our room chief, Czech I think, told us the rules of use in French. Then in small groups that we formed ourselves, according to our own wishes, we took possession of our bedding. We received a paper sleeping bag. The room was a veritable scaffold. Struts everywhere formed wooden beds. Bunks built to military measurements were in rows of three arranged in three tiers. The distance between one tier and the next meant you could sit down. Only the top tier didn't have enough room for this. A clean well-filled straw mattress allowed us enough rest. Having to sleep very close together was made bearable thanks to the chill of the night air.

During the daytime, the room was forbidden to us. We stayed in the yard. It was the same size as the building and was also flanked by another building identical to ours. These huts, all identical, extended over 300 metres and only comprised a very small part of the camp.

In the morning, reveille was sounded at four-thirty. At five o'clock we were outside. There we shivered. The tepid fake coffee was not enough to warm us up. We huddled together in vain. The wind whistled through the yard, mocking our attempts to stay warm. Some jumped up and down, did windmills with their arms, but soon breathless and shivering constantly, they suffered in silence and waited not so much for sunrise, bitterly cold in this region, but for the warm time of the day when the sun's rays would finally chase away this freezing atmosphere. At nine o'clock, the chill replaced the cold; at ten o'clock the warmth replaced the chill. This was the perfect moment when the mild warmth reminded us of the spring that we had left behind. Up until midday the effect of the sun was beneficial.

Meantime, we had been served soup. It arrived without warning but was always welcome. The size of the camp's population meant the kitchens were always busy and it wasn't possible to have a fixed timetable. When the last man had been served, it was the turn of the first man. The afternoons were unbearable – the opposite of the mornings but just as intense. When the sun was at its zenith there was no shade at all. Along the walls, the so-called 'sheltered' space offered scarcely any comfort and we were all forced to endure what we were, in truth, fervently wishing for throughout the morning.

Faced with our inability to fight this unavoidable evil, we submitted to it. The stony ground was soon completely covered with stretched-out bodies. Each man was forced to sunbathe, lying on his jacket with his naked torso and head covered with a shirt. If you turned over frequently, the heat was less intense. Even so, after a few days, you began to see some strange-looking heads; swollen, with puffy eyelids, the eyes completely hidden, these heads looked more like balloons. Thankfully, this almost spontaneous swelling was not painful. It lasted for a few days, improved a bit and disappeared.

Our first days in this tight space were monotonous. The arrival of the soup, morning and evening, was the single wished-for moment. The night no longer offered any attraction for it led almost immediately to the pale and frozen morning. Our only consolation was to be able to quench our thirst at any hour of the day or night. The water, crystal-clear and icy, was always available to us. During those first days, trying to control our wish to drink, the unit boss deliberately recommended that we drink little: this water was impure and contained some microbe or other. I have no idea whether this was true or a lie, but I never held back and I never suffered from it.

By some irony, we finally had to undergo a medical visit. Body measurements, weight, X-rays, the consultation was thorough. Some of us even learned in this very place the disease we were suffering from. Those with tuberculosis were put back into buildings separated from the rest of the camp. They didn't work anymore or very little and were fed a special diet. I don't know if these therapeutic measures went on for very long… Then we made another visit to the *Effektenkammer* [clothes storage room] and were dressed up as forced labourers. We were now ready to set off for work, after having sewn our registration badge and the red triangle bearing the initial of our nationality on to both jacket, at heart level, and the left trouser leg, just under the pocket.

•

A convoy of 100 men was formed. I was one unit of that convoy. We made our way on foot to a work camp 9km away near Munich. Our march was tough and lasted around two hours. We could see the camp. It looked even less inviting than the one we had just left. While the entrance was less impressive, it nevertheless demanded more solemnity. We had to fall into line, our heads bare too. As we walked by, several Krauts to the right and to the left of the narrow entryway monitored us, our pace, our hairstyles. Slaps and kicks seemed to be par for the course.

The situation felt as if it were getting worse and worse. The cloud-filled sky itself contributed to our great unhappiness. The fog seemed to draw an impenetrable veil over this tragic piece of ground. It seemed to want to conceal from the innocent twinkling stars a vision that nature itself frowned upon. An extended courtyard led off the entrance. We came to a halt. We were searched. Blows landed. A penknife here or a spoon there were enough to provoke anger, shouting and punishments all at the same time.

From here we proceeded to a building still being constructed. Barbers were waiting for us. We were branded with a central parting from front to back, the width of a razor. Those whose hair was still very short felt the razor's burn. The parting was then even more obvious. Thus prepared, we were deployed in different cellblocks. The central part was made of wood. The cellblock boss, a civil law prisoner, received us with no fuss and no words. It was beginning to get dark even though it wasn't very late, but the mist was getting thicker.

A mournful bell sounded suddenly, surprising us as we were adjusting to our surroundings. Immediately afterwards, the boss's whistle warned us of the roll call. We had to move quickly. A rapid headcount was taken on the threshold of our block. Then in columns of ten, we moved towards the big square. It was about 18:30 hours. From every direction, actual regiments of men approached. Each one in step. Grunts, yells, threats were dished out by different bosses who were furiously trying to line them up perfectly.

Finally, each cellblock from the first to the twentieth, even the thirtieth perhaps, was in its place. Everything got a lot more serious. The line-up, ten rows deep, was supposed to be straight. The shouting intensified accompanied by blows this time. I had a sudden astonishing realisation at this point. The *Kapos*, the cellblock bosses, all of them ranked prisoners, were possessed of an indescribable brutality. I could barely understand this wickedness among brothers in misery. Yet it was a fact and I frequently had the misfortune to experience it.

Our assembly was impeccable. We expected the goodwill of these men. Suddenly a roar, which was an order, warned us that the roll call was about to begin. A petty officer was visible. What this order was, I have no idea. Have I forgotten it? Did I ever understand it? Brief commands, distant at first, then coming nearer and nearer, rang out at regular intervals in the silence. It was the cell boss who ordered us to stand still as the Krauts approached. As he got up to the top of the first row, he issued the order *Mutzen ab* [caps off]. Quick headcount. Then once he had gone beyond the last row, the order to stand at ease and *Mutzen auf* [caps on] meant we could stand easy.

This twice-daily headcount, mornings and evenings, took place at set times whatever the weather. Its duration depended on the mood of the designated guard of the day and especially on the state of the weather. The rain, the snow, the icy wind all affected how long it lasted. How sweet, how good it was, from the vantage point of an over-heated room, how gratifying to be present at the spectacle of several thousand shivering men, powerless in the rain. Their futile attempts to shield themselves from the freezing wind no doubt caused sniggers of satisfaction.

And in winter, this great dark blot on this muddied carpet of snow must have been a great sight. The first roll call was enough to make us imagine how hard this new German camp, our second, was going to be. After this first backbreaking day, the end of the evening's roll call made me breathe out with a sense of ease, especially since the evening meal would follow right away.

Once we got back to the cellblock, the food was given out by cubicle. Our diet consisted of some black bread – which didn't contain a single grain of wheat flour – a piece of sausage or margarine, a few boiled potatoes. I gobbled it down voraciously. Night had fallen. Feeble electric light lit our imminent bedtime. I undressed and stretched out.

I was giving in to sleep when once again a whistle sounded. I sat up, worried and curious. Our room boss responsible for his barracks wanted to be certain of his new workforce. A headcount would satisfy him. Oh how tedious this was. The first time, several were missing, then the actual number was higher than the notional number. Finally, he had to do partial headcounts by nationality to land on the exact number. By this time, an hour had gone by. At 22:00 hours we were finally able to lie down on our straw mattresses for a short night's sleep. I quickly dozed off and still remember sleeping soundly. The gloomy hoarse sound of the feeble siren would not have been enough to wake me up. But our vigilant bulldog armed with an alarm set it off ahead of time. The signal, a brutal *aufstehen* [get up], aroused panic. We had to get up immediately. The few who hesitated were thrown roughly to the ground from the second or third tier of bunks. Then, bare chested, we had to go to the wash basins outside. The icy cold of the edge of night held us in its grip. It was four-thirty in the morning, dawn itself was not making an appearance. Our only solace was a cup of tepid coffee. At six o'clock, a new alarm, a new whistle for the morning roll call. Dawn was piercing the shadows of the night. The intensity of the cold was made worse by an icy wind. The roll call was the same as the night before, same shouts, same orders, same signs of respect shown to the hated one.

Then the various *Kommandos* [work squads] got into groups. We were new without any particular assignments. We were allocated according to what was required – some to kitchen duties, or to cleaning, others to toilet duties, or as reinforcements in work units where staff numbers were reduced through illness. These unexpected duties inside the camp were not too arduous. Some were even sought after – spud-bashing duties, for example – because it meant you got one or two extra rations of soup. Toilet duties were not looked down on despite the stinking load to be transported and the splashes of shit. You could carry out each load quite slowly and break up each trip with numerous stops.

We were allocated these lightweight jobs for a few days. Then we were given serious employment. Most of my comrades had to work in an aircraft factory about 3 or 4km from the camp. Personally, I was part of an open-air *Kommando*. We were building a camp outbuilding adjacent to and outside our camp. Several buildings made from rough stones were already up. Others were in the process of construction. Many teams were sharing the work among themselves: bricklayers, carpenters, electricians, joiners and especially labourers – who went from one team to another as required. Here too, luck played its part. Feeding the mechanical concrete mixer, carrying the cement, was an exhausting job. You had to follow the relentless rhythm of the cement mixer.

At nine o'clock in the morning, we got a snack. At nine-fifteen, work started again. At midday we went back to the camp where we had our daily soup – thin runny soup devoid of any meat – downing it in a few minutes. At twelve-thirty, each group went back to its place of work. For a fortnight I was subjected to this harsh work of the labourer and as such, I worked successively in all aspects of the building trade.

I will always remember a couple of slaps handed out to me by a trainee Polish *Kapo*, which made me weep tears of impotent rage. I was supposed to make mortar by hand. I wasn't very skilful at turning my shovel and mixed the cement very badly. Apparently, it looked like I was trying to sabotage the work. So it was that suddenly a rough hand crashed down on me. I faced my provoker in a fury but without any thought of retaliation. The *Kapos*, our overseers, were unquestionably the strongest. Well nourished, not forced to do brutal work, their fundamental job was to make us suffer. They certainly never had to be whipped to carry out their grim task more effectively.

This vast enterprise was patrolled by a soldier with a weapon slung over his shoulder and always accompanied by a glossy-coated German Shepherd dog with a cat-like prowl and eager to bite. This brute's role was to watch that everyone was working. The role of each prisoner was not to let himself be caught out doing nothing, at least when our own supervisors were not there to maintain the pace. However, sometimes we were taken by surprise, leaning on the handles of our spade or pickaxe. Then, the zealous guard would raise his arms and launch himself into our group, hitting us very hard, while the dog would join in biting here, biting there. The madman would stop once he'd worn himself out. The surveillance *Kapo* was reprimanded for our laziness and we started work again at a faster pace while being beaten and shouted at.

The work finally stopped at 18:00 hours. Evening roll call, soup, team checks all kept us on our toes until gone 21:00 hours. Then we were allowed to sleep. Many of my comrades slept badly or very little. Bedbugs and fleas constantly bothered them. I was lucky enough not to feel anything and every evening I fell deeply asleep.

The next day we were met with the same routine. Just the job was different. Instead of the shovel and the pickaxe, we had to push the wagons, sift sand, level a plot of land, install or move a narrow-gauge rail track, carry beams etc, etc. Work was never interrupted by poor weather; the frequent rain common in this region wet us through and through. Then, soaked to the bone, we shivered in the crisp air even in the middle of July. Our only good moments came when there was an air-raid warning, which occurred often at that time.

The signal for an approaching warning was given to us by the emission of an artificial fog in the vicinity of the neighbouring factory. The siren went off quite quickly. We gathered rapidly into groups and made our way at a swift pace to the shelters inside the camp. The fog then invaded our camp. You could hear a distant rumbling, growing more and more distinct, and soon, to our great joy, the bombing began. The more violent it was, the longer it went on, the greater was our satisfaction. Not only was imminent justice on the horizon, but first and foremost, we appreciated the unexpected and unscheduled boon of respite from work.

The length of these air-raid warnings varied from half an hour to more than two hours. Even during the night, we were sometimes woken up abruptly. We found it hard to leave a warm mattress for a cold, damp shelter. We had to, not because it was wiser to do so but because that was the rule. Our camp, well demarcated, could not be the object of any premeditated attack. It was the best possible shelter. Only a stray bomb could reach it – which was an extremely rare occurrence.

EIGHT

THE HANGINGS

Prisoners of war were put to work by most nations fighting in the Second World War. This was in accordance with the Geneva Convention of 1929. However, both Japan and Germany organised huge forced labour regimes, in violation of international law. And while they both put civilians to work in the occupied territories, Germany outdid Japan on the deportation of foreign civilians, prisoners of war and concentration camp inmates into the Reich to work for Germany's war effort. Very few worked voluntarily, and their working conditions varied, depending on their origins. The Nazis operated a sliding scale, with humans from Scandinavia, the Netherlands and Flanders at the top of the pile – Nordic and Germanic, thus 'Aryan', and the rest divided into Axis and non-Axis aliens. The Poles, Soviet citizens, gypsies and Jews were at the bottom of the scale. The Jews and gypsies faced extermination.[40]

Within this warped but rigorously ordered hierarchy, the French were neither fully Aryan, nor subhuman. They haunted the middle ground in this artificially constructed universe of terror.

---

40 Spoerer, Mark, and Jochen Fleischhacker. 'Forced Labourers in Nazi Germany: Categories, Numbers and Survivors'. *The Journal of Interdisciplinary History*, Vol. 33, no. 2, 2002, pp. 169–204. JSTOR, http://www.jstor.org/stable/3656586

FROM ROLAND'S MEMOIR

Each prisoner's constant thought was how to escape, but this was not possible for political detainees. Not only was physical impairment a significant obstacle, but the striped uniform, the haircut, the lack of any food supplies, almost always made any attempt pointless. Finally, and above all, the punishment if you didn't succeed was such that most of the prisoners submitted to the awful life of the camps. Any attempt to escape was punished with death by hanging. At the beginning, I don't think we really believed they would do this, but after seeing several prisoners hanged in front of the entire camp, we soon understood this was indeed the punishment.

I had been walking on German soil for about a month when I had the misfortune to be present at the hanging of two Russians. When we got back from work at midday, pushing through the crowd at roll call, we saw that two holes had been dug several metres away. Next to them, two gibbets lay on their side, not leaving any doubt about the scaffolding being built. Indeed, at 18:00 hours the gibbets were raised. At 18:30 hours the roll call took place, quickly this time. It wasn't difficult to guess that the pathetic spectacle of two hangings was reserved for us, no doubt as a warning.

The condemned men appeared, two strong lads, one very tall, the other of medium height but very sturdily built. Surrounded by a dozen Krauts, holding submachine guns, dogs on leads, their fate wasn't in doubt. No help could come their way. Booted officers, holding riding whips, were talking and joking. They didn't seem to understand the gravity of the moment. Not only were two human lives going to be scrubbed out, but this inhuman, unjust and illegal act should put an entire people beyond the bounds of humanity. For a generation at least, this act should cause this perverted, limited, insensitive, pitiless people to be blacklisted by all civilised nations.

The two Russians approached, straight-backed, heads held high, without weakness. A stepladder was placed under each gallows. A prisoner read the death sentence. Different interpreters translated into the most commonly spoken languages: Russian, Polish, French, Czech. The text stated explicitly that the hanging was not punishment for attempting to escape, but for looting on German soil which the two foreigners were guilty of. No one was fooled. The executions were not simultaneous. One of them, the tall one, climbed the stepladder. The noose was put around his neck. He said a few words in Russian. The stepladder was overturned and a life was broken. The second condemned man was hanged in the same way. His last words were brutally cut short by the rope. The first man had said 'Farewell Russians, farewell Russia'. Brief words that prove vividly that the mother country is not a meaningless phrase. And that your compatriots, however crazy and mean they might be, are nevertheless the least unbearable, the least unsociable of companions. The two hanged bodies received a final farewell from all the deportees – a silent farewell, unwittingly allowed.

On these dark occasions, the crowd didn't split up as usual into twenty or thirty groups. A procession took place in front of the corpses. This was not a final honour that we might be offering up with warmth, but rather that cynical taste for drawing out a morbid spectacle. We believed this double crime to be the sacrifice of two innocent lives to German savagery. The German gods wanted human blood. For five years already, they had been drinking this blood and their bloodthirsty spirit had never ceased to deepen.

The two Russians will always stay in my memory as two hanged men. Their death was courageous and dignified. I don't think it caused anyone to have any nightmares. This dramatic spectacle could only reveal to us our desire to survive in order one day to expose all the wickedness, all the ignominy of the German civilisation.

We knew that escape was impossible, but our willingness to resist the beatings, the cold, the hunger was growing stronger. We knew how to submit, we knew how to brave the elements, but we also knew how to handle empty shovels, spy on our surroundings, hide in the latrines and stay there for a while. If you were caught red-handed, you were hit, but fifteen or twenty minutes of rest was worth a couple of slaps in the face or several lashes of the whip. In this terrible place, the punishments were not proportionate to the misdeeds.

I remember a quarryman who was on the receiving end of fifteen lashes from a riding whip and whose backside was subsequently covered with bluish-red stripes. He had been busy carrying mortar throughout the day. After work, worn out with fatigue, he climbed into his bunk on the top tier and fell deeply asleep. He hadn't told anyone. The roll call was sounded, the first headcount took place, someone was missing. This was a frequent occurrence. The cellblock boss knew it and everyone in the barracks came back to his designated place. The numbers then would always be right.

On that day, the missing person did not turn up. The boss responsible goes back to the cellblock after waiting impatiently for ten minutes, makes a hurried search of the beds but doesn't find anyone. He comes back in time to greet the day's officer and tell him that someone is absent. Short discussion during which it was doubtless recognised that escape was unlikely, the roll call continued and our boss returned to the block to make a more thorough search. The roll call ended. We knew by hearsay that any getaway attempt meant we would have to stay standing for several hours. The authorities effectively only allowed us to return to the block when the cause of the absence had been clearly established. But on this occasion, we assumed the truth which was quickly confirmed.

Our unfortunate comrade soon appeared, barely awake and also a bit dazed because of the blows he had received; he scurried in front of the cellblock chief. This first violent and crude punishment was not enough. Summoned to the guardhouse the following day, he explained the completely warranted and very plausible reasons for his absence, but in vain. He was sentenced to twenty-five lashes of the whip. This punishment was administered on the same day, in the evening after the roll call. A table had been brought for this purpose. He had to lie down on it, with his legs hanging. His only protection was a lightweight pair of trousers. A non-commissioned officer (NCO) approached. In his hand he held a whip designed for these occasions – it was long, flexible, thin at the end, wide at the handle. The NCO straightened himself up, lifted his arm and drew it back, and with all his force, all his energy, all his brutishness, he brought his whip down onto the loins of our unfortunate friend.

On the third lash, screams of pain resounded. This encouraged the brute. The blows became ever more fierce, the entire body was pulled up onto tiptoes. I was astonished to see this enthusiasm for hitting; the screams became moans, the moaning turned to groans. On the fifteenth lash, the officer in charge who was probably enjoying the show, judged the punishment sufficient. The assailant was out of breath and sweating. He mopped his forehead, proud of having accomplished his despicable task.

The next day during the daytime we were able to observe the long streaks of blue, black and red which criss-crossed the offender's lower back and backside. I wasn't surprised. The vigour with which the lashes were meted out could not have any other result.

This second experience only served to confirm our intention to skive off as much as possible. Whip lashes carried out quickly, and with conviction but without skill, to punish an accidental nap, were better than punishment delivered methodically for an offence committed because of painful, prolonged work on some building site. Individual jobs caused me to suffer numerous slaps, but in the evening, at the longed-for time, I wasn't exhausted. I still had sufficient resources to endure more than two hours of standing upright.

One job I hated was filling and transporting the trolleys. This transport was done in a single train. Several teams, one per wagon, worked together. Not everyone had the spirit of passive resistance to the same degree. Despite our efforts to facilitate a level of productivity that was quite low, but that was regular and general, we always found that certain groups were stupid enough to finish their job before the others. They made the most of an extra rest but obliged us to speed up our pace, and on the next trip we had to take the zeal of fellow teammates into account. The gaps in productivity were even more significant when the teams formed were not homogeneous. The foreigners did not form efficient groups among themselves. Each man reproached the other for his slow pace or his half-full shovels. The time lost to these sterile discussions then had to be made up with rigorous effort which was very painful for under-nourished men. Sometimes, even an individual job – rubble clearance or backfilling – was carried out by a group. In this group, some went at an unintentional and unjustified pace, others went slowly but steadily, while the last ones, faithful to their principles, faced the slaps and, where necessary, accepted them philosophically.

The first group was blamed by the two other categories; the second, either through jealousy or stupidity, blamed the third group as well. This last group incited the weak ones to imitate their example and strove in vain to justify their conduct to the second group. And collectively, no one suffered at all from this sabotage. The work required several weeks to carry out and no daily limit could be fixed. And besides, the punishment was individual and only applied to the offender. My own experience allows me to claim that it was only this latter behaviour – taking rest where possible – that was likely to preserve a modicum of strength. Each time I had the chance to apply my method, I finished up the day in a satisfactory state. But unfortunately, when I couldn't do this, which was more often the case, I was exhausted in the evening.

My work placement as all-purpose labourer lasted about three weeks. Then I was part of a *Kommando* of about fifty men. And without knowing what was waiting for me, I was happy to leave behind me this godforsaken place where I had been cold in the middle of July, where I had been hungry, where I had endured every evil thing both physically and emotionally – where, finally, I had suffered more in twenty-one days than a man might suffer in ten years of a normal existence. I didn't think there was a harder life that could be the lot of human beings than the one that I had just been living through.

NINE

EISENACH

The small city of Eisenach, Roland's next destination, is in the state of Thuringia in central Germany. Johann Sebastian Bach was born there. Martin Luther spent his childhood in Eisenach. It is where engineering firm BMW now runs its smallest plant, designing and producing tools and large exterior body parts for its Rolls-Royce vehicles.

BMW became one of the most important companies in Germany's armaments industry, producing aero-engines. Its two plants in Munich and Eisenach, producing motorcycles and automobiles respectively, couldn't cope with the huge volume of aero-engines demanded by the Third Reich for the rearmament of the Luftwaffe, the German air force. The government funded the construction of two plants in 1936 and 1937, Munich-Allach and Eisenach-Dürrerhof, both heavily camouflaged to look like part of the forest. As production increased and the economy soared on the back of Germany's rearmament, the need for labour also soared.

At the end of 1939, BMW was using Polish prisoners of war in Eisenach. BMW was recruiting workers from the occupied territories, from other Axis countries and also from western and southern Europe. The latter were better treated, with similar rights to German workers. The pecking order based on origins remained intact: concentration camp inmates, prisoners and workers from the east at the bottom of the pile. As the war continued, those non-German workers with more privileges saw their rights disappear, the differences between groups diminished, labour became forced labour for everyone. Living conditions grew ever grimmer, food ever more scarce.[41]

By the end of 1944, forced labourers made up over 50 per cent of the workforce, some 29,000 workers. Roland was one of them.

Nevertheless, even at this late stage of the war, compared with Dachau, life at the Eisenach factory was marginally more bearable for Roland, with slightly more to eat and more time for sleeping.

•

FROM ROLAND'S MEMOIR

I was ignorant and lucky to be assigned to a factory *Kommando* where the gradual loss of strength took place slowly and without daily clashes. One evening, we were warned we would be leaving the next morning at four o'clock. We sighed with contentment. Once again, we made our meagre preparations. For the first time since we had set foot on German soil, we were offered tobacco, as long as we paid for it of course. I was poorer than a beggar and didn't know how to get hold of the few marks that the tobacco cost. I didn't know the exchange rate for this product otherwise I certainly would have pushed to obtain the few francs I needed.

We were woken up by our cellblock boss whom we left behind without any regrets. A day's worth of supplies was given out to us and at four-thirty in the morning we were assembled in front of the guard post near the main exit through which we had come, bare-headed and in step, still ignorant of the Nazis' instincts. A search was carried out after a half-hour of waiting around. Penknives were found, slaps were handed out. There was the sound of an engine. Two buses appeared. To our great astonishment, they were for us. We were then driven to Munich station. There we had the honour once again of travelling in a passenger compartment. Dawn was beginning to break when the train moved off. Around fifteen soldiers were guarding us. The unexpected comfort of this journey surprised us. Once we were settled, everyone dozed off. I really welcomed this trip as it meant

....
41 https://www.bmwgroup.com/en/company/history/BMW-during-the-era-of-national-socialism.html

a nice long period of rest. The noise, the jolting could not disturb our sleep in any way.

Daylight, however, woke us up. We were able to look at the German countryside at our leisure. It left us unmoved. None of it reminded us of our meadows, our fields, our waves of wheat. It seemed hard, unattractive, uninviting. It matched the people that it nourished. The grazing land seemed to suffocate under the high grass, dense and thick. The ploughing didn't have that diversity of colours that ours did. It revealed black, greasy soil. The forests only had one type of tree: the pine. What's more, they seemed artificial because they all looked the same. That day, I was able to have breakfast but only through giving up my main meal of the day. This journey was a moment of peace in the ordeal that was beginning for us.

We didn't suffer any harassment for the entire day; we could even see ourselves as passengers. Our clothes and our haircuts were the only things that reminded us of the sad truth. Even the soldiers took no notice of us. During the afternoon, we formed choirs. The Russians led the way and sang some popular songs. Their songs with their slow rhythm, their narrow range, their low notes perfectly matched our state of mind. They asked us to join in. We began with a few well-known songs, then we sang the *Marseillaise*. We were just finishing it when the leader of the soldiers' detail came up to us to ask us in a friendly way to choose another song.

He could do no less and we complied. There was a little platform at the front of the train. I even had the pleasure of going there to shake out my jacket. A young soldier played a few popular French songs for us on his harmonica. I was grateful to him at that moment for his interest in our country. But now I wonder what misdeeds he could have carried out, or even just been present at as an indifferent spectator.

•

We reached our intended destination quite late. At the station's exit there was a bus waiting for us – we were certainly visitors of note – which took us via many detours to our objective, the BMW factory at Eisenach. Complete darkness, the night black as ink, meant that we couldn't get a glimpse of this factory. We went into a vast well-lit workshop where we were assailed first of all by a smell of oil. Our arrival aroused the curiosity of the night workers, most of them prisoners, who came up to us to get a closer look. Then, after advancing another 100 metres, we came to the back of the factory. There was the cellblock. A single door separated the factory from our living quarters. Lights went on in the block, which was usually dark at this late hour. Those sleeping there were soon awoken by this untimely brightness, and they sat on their beds staring at us.

Their curiosity was shared.

We were struck by the faces of our future companions, sitting up under the crude light of powerful electric lamps. They looked drained, with a yellowish cadaverous pallor. Yet they seemed neither too thin nor too weak. Most of them, their chests bare, didn't have the skeletal bodies that we found later. When we discovered the daily diet, it seemed to us plentiful compared to the one we had just left behind. We were hoping that soup would arrive to crown this unique day but no pot was to be seen and nothing led us to believe that we were expected.

After a roll call, we were effectively challenged to find a bed that was unoccupied in this huge dormitory with three tiers of beds. We managed to do so with difficulty. Several men had to sleep in pairs. The French prisoners had told us that theft was rife in these places. Those who had a bit of money, some food or some tobacco, hid their wealth as best they could under the threadbare bolster or under the mattress, while the most careful even slept in their trousers so they could keep their precious tobacco on them. Then we didn't waste any time in falling deeply asleep.

The next morning at five-thirty, the light and the fateful *aufstehen* [get up] woke us up. At first, we were surprised – and pleasantly – to realise that the command to get up was not followed by a general commotion; many dawdled for five, ten and even fifteen minutes before deciding to get out of their bed. None of the violent reactions which we were used to. Another surprise too – this time extremely unpleasant – was finding out about the night-time thieving which all the French were victims of. What curses followed an otherwise hopeful wake-up call, but there was no getting around the stealing and there was no point in thinking you would ever find these small supplies, the handful of marks or the precious tobacco. Others had a field day without any remorse. Our consolation was to be able to stay in bed; it was even a duty. At about five to six a whistle was blown. It was the order for the day's workers to gather. The number was fixed. No absence was allowed in the morning. Then at six o'clock, a gloomy siren sounded. It was the end of the night shift, the resumption of the morning shift. A noise of multiple, resonating footsteps preceded the return to the cellblock of the prisoners we had seen the evening before. They were replaced immediately; then they went to bed after drinking a coffee.

Day began to break. We rested in the expectation of daylight which would allow us to get to know our new home.

The favourable impression that we had picked up from the journey was confirmed by the location and design of our block. It was divided into two parts lengthwise, but not separated. One side was reserved for sleeping; another for daily life. On this side next to the wall there was a line of tables and benches and some small cupboards side by side standing against the wall.

These two sections with different uses allowed room for a covered aisle, quite narrow but long enough. It was there that we gathered several times a day, five rows deep.

One end had been reserved for a sick bay, washbasins and toilets. You got to the toilets by going past the washbasins. These rooms were separated by a partition wall and benefitted from a ceiling. You went in via an ordinary canvas curtain. The toilets had a dozen seats with running water.

The other end abutted directly onto the wall. A high, wide window at chin height allowed us to see outside, although unfortunately it was covered with a wire mesh. My stay in this enclosed place lasted six months. It was unventilated but protected us from the bad weather and the cold spells to come. The timetable that was imposed upon us and which never varied is fixed in my memory for life. The places themselves will never be forgotten. I will always recall that vast hall populated with machines that were all quite similar and which were going night and day. The roof was made of curved reinforced concrete arches, joined together by a vertical glass wall through which the sunlight reached us. At night the blackout curtains were placed in front of these huge glass panels. Vents were fixed at regular intervals in the walls. During the summer, these vents were blowing the cooler outside air; in the winter they would blow warm air, or so we assumed.

The siren went off again. It was midday. The current shift was returning to the block to get their daily soup. (At half-past midday, back to work.)

The moment they arrived, yesterday's labourers, rapidly promoted, rushed to their usual tables. Each man had his spoon and his bowl, which looked like a chamber pot but with more splayed edges; it could hold about a litre and a half. Once each table was filled up, the cellblock boss did a quick headcount to detect if there were any freeloaders after soup. Then the *Stubendienst* [room service], or more precisely, the head of the kitchen staff got on with distributing the soup. He was a big lad from Siberia, well proportioned, high cheekbones, slanted eyes, thunderous voice. He alternated between one end and the other of the line of tables. When he made a mistake, he was quickly called to order by the interested parties! It only took him half an hour to distribute 150–200 portions. Of course, the last served only had ten minutes to consume their soup, wash out their bowl and put it in the cupboard. This very limited amount of time was enough though. At half-past midday: form into groups, headcount and the siren announcing the return to the factory.

During the next few days that passed we were able to enjoy our complete freedom, within the limits of the cellblock. We were not subjected to any work. Our occupations were chatting, reading a few dull novels and primarily sleeping. Then from time to time we had to carry out a few chores, more or less difficult, more or less long. Our leisure moments were still plentiful. Then there were certain postings. A group of our comrades was sent to a neighbouring factory. I didn't see them again. Several among us received postings and from the next day had to obey the inflexible timetable. About twenty of us didn't have definite jobs. The chores multiplied and not a day went by without us having to interrupt our snoozing or our reading. This way of life was still preferable to that of the worker. Finally, successive partial withdrawals of some of our number meant the end of our workforce. Three or four didn't have the advantage of a 'specialised' job and after a few months were sent to the central camp at Buchenwald.

On this occasion again I had luck on my side. First of all, I benefitted from a late assignment, and then I had the good fortune to be part of 'Quality Control' and one morning I found myself seated on a stool in front of a table. My professional partner was an Austrian with a very poor knowledge of French. Yet we understood each other. The work consisted of checking the parts that the machines were fabricating in large quantities under the supervision of our companions. In this job, I was lucky to stay on the day shift for more than two months. I could therefore rest peacefully from seven or eight o'clock in the evening to half-past five in the morning. Like the great majority, I took my time getting up. I had quickly judged how long I needed for my morning ablutions, dressing and breakfast. This consisted of a third of a litre of coffee served in our bowls. Coffee substitute, no sugar – I quickly abandoned it. The teams alternated each week. We had Sundays off. This was a privilege that wasn't granted to us but was obligatory because the factory's workforce included some free workers and Germans. They held the supervisory and leadership jobs. Among them you found young people doubtless not suitable for military service and old people, real soldiers but not worthy of respect.

Twice a week, the day shift profited from an outing in the fresh air. At six o'clock we were taken to a disused yard. It was bordered along two long sides by two massive buildings that were identical to ours, while width-wise it was bordered by a narrow building that connected the other two. Along the other length a simple barbed wire fence separated us from the outside world – I was going to say, from liberty, but using this word on German soil is a misnomer. We were strictly forbidden from approaching this side, which attracted us greatly because the pure country air reached us more directly; four or five guards stationed along less than 50 metres made sure that we respected the order.

The fine days then meant we could go outside. We went out bare-chested and shook out our ragged clothes. Some even organised team games. Aware of my debilitated state, maybe not visible to others, I abstained from physical exercise and contented myself with filling my lungs with air and walking in the company of a few good comrades. Unfortunately, this genuine breathing exercise only lasted for half an hour. On Sunday afternoons, we stayed outside for one or two hours. The menu was slightly better on that day. The soup was more fatty, the vegetables more abundant. Our leisure time then was devoted to sleeping and laundry. The Russians often broke into song.

We liked their nostalgic songs at first. Then this constant repetition of the rhythm, the same intonations over and over again, made the tune intolerable. We didn't have the same musical perceptions. But nevertheless, I did come to sympathise with some of the Russians. It was only possible when we worked in close proximity and communicated with each other by speaking in German, which we hated equally. I even made efforts to learn this semi-Asiatic language. The grammar didn't seem too detailed and seemed less complex than ours; the pronunciation wasn't too tricky, just a few letters were hard for us to say.

Unfortunately, my memory had followed the downward spiral of my physical health and it was with difficulty that I strove to retain ten or fifteen common words every day. I even learnt to count but my memory was not sufficiently resilient. As for my willpower, I was totally concentrating on life, intent every day on hanging on to as much strength, as much energy, as possible.

Every week, the day shift was taken to the showers. On this occasion, our underwear – underpants and shirt – were changed. This sanitary measure took place every week and it was always welcomed. However, the water was not always warm enough. Soap was replaced with a powder which must have been caustic soda. The amount of time allowed was too strictly limited. I was often dead last to finish, despite my normal dexterity in getting dressed.

Over the summer the lice visits began. Before we went down to the showers located in a dimly lit basement, a male nurse examined our private parts by the muted light of a torch. The 'barber' was waiting for those whose body hair had grown, or those on whom a few lice had been detected by the alerted eye of our health officer. The result of this observation was conclusive. Every time, more and more lousy men were discovered. And a disinfecting session was set up each week.

This took place in a building situated in the centre of town and prompted, aside from the compulsory shower, a supplementary renewal of underwear and a Sunday procession in town. As the lice problem got worse, it was finally decided to disinfect everyone completely. One Sunday, our workforce was divided into two groups. As dawn broke, the first group left equipped with blankets; I was part of it. The chilly morning made us shiver at first, but the blankets draped around our shoulders to protect against the cold soon warmed us up as we walked. It took about an hour of walking quite slowly to get to our destination.

When we got there nothing was ready. The fire wasn't even lit. We had to stay outside.

It was going to be a very fine day – the sky hinted at an azure blue. The first yellow-red rays of the rising sun were dispersing the light curtain of mist. In any other circumstance, the spectacle would have been sublime. The barbarity of our uniforms, the stupidity of our masters, the massive graceless buildings – everything, in a word, made by the Germans – contrasted with nature. The sun began its diurnal journey. The rays reached us more directly. We felt an inexpressible sense of well-being. We quickly threw off our blankets to feel the sun on our shoulders. Then we sat down and stretched out. A sustained caress seemed intent on making us forget our present suffering. What a memorable moment!

The base physical necessities brought us back to our objective. The showers had been heated up, along with the furnaces; we had to take all our clothes off in the small yard in the fresh air, bundle up our rags and finally enter a narrow dirty lobby area. We were offered an excellent shower.

A small bar of substitute soap handed out to each of us guaranteed we had a good clean. We were given clean underwear, that is, undershirt and underpants. Dressed thus, we went back to the small courtyard. The sun had continued on its way. It was darting out hot rays now. Over an hour later, the disinfection of our uniform and our blankets had been completed. The bundles were in a heap outside and each man had to look for his own belongings. The midday siren had rung out a while ago by the time we were ready to return to our lodgings. It was a difficult walk back because of the heat, scorching by then. Our blankets were quite a burden. We finally arrived, thirsty but especially starving. We easily quenched our thirst. On the other hand, there were no hoped-for billycans to assuage our hunger. The second group was supposed to come after us for disinfection and the meal was supposed to take place once they came back. There was only one thing for it: go to bed.

Unfortunately, our mattresses, our bolsters, our bedding had not been cleaned so we came back to a cellblock that was just as dirty as we had left it. And despite the massacre, not all the lice had perished. It would not be long before they multiplied and covered us again. This partial procedure slowed down their return but did not stop the danger. A few hours' sleep brought us towards the evening. The bright day was beginning to lose its brilliance when the second convoy of disinfected men arrived. This session had been relatively fast. Finally, at 18:00 hours our lunch was served, followed immediately by our supper. Unconcerned about the future and despite the relative abundance of the meal, I devoured the whole menu in less than half an hour. I confess to having a full stomach that evening.

Yet my sleep was uninterrupted and not at all upset by indigestion. The next morning, my hunger was no more satisfied than on previous days. The food contained very little nutritional value. To keep up our strength, we would have needed a diet five times as plentiful or five times more nutritious. Even so, up until this point, our weight loss wasn't so pronounced. The most highly coloured complexions lost their bloom bit by bit, becoming pale and yellow-tinted. Extremely fat bodies melted away, slightly fat bodies grew smaller, those with very little fat stayed the same. Everyone, however, lost muscle tone and energy. Personally, being of medium height but quite muscular I did not lose much weight, but each day I lost a little of the wonderful energy of my athletic, hot-blooded youth. My matt skin tone grew paler, whiter. Our scrawny condition, maybe not obvious, seemed to be ignored by the many skin troubles which are the sign of an over-rich diet. I've never had fewer spots.

During this summer period, in this unhealthy, even sordid place, I only caught a kind of scabies which spread over the thighs and lower abdomen. It was eradicated quite quickly by an oily yellowish liquid of unknown composition. A good mate caught jaundice; only his skin colour revealed what was wrong. He was admitted to the sick bay but didn't receive any care there. His diet was not improved at all, just the amount reduced. He wasn't allowed margarine or sausage. He had to be satisfied with eating his dry bread. Ultimately, the jaundice seemed to disappear of its own accord. The disease emaciated and weakened my friend who, six months later, finished up his time as a deportee worn out and at the end of his tether. It took him more than a year to recover his mental health and still today he has to be careful about his physical health.

The doctor for our *Kommando* was Czech, quite young. He had no medical experience at all; our camp was the first time he had a chance to practise medicine. He didn't exert himself to make up for this lack of experience. Deprived of the necessary drugs, he thought any personal effort was a waste of time. And yet he could have been more generous in offering the *Schonung* [protection] which was so highly appreciated. A few days' rest would often have been a tonic not only for physical health but also for mental health. In short, our amateur quack's interests lay in reducing the number of patients who no doubt bothered him in the sick bay where he had his own bed. With this in mind, he didn't accept many patients or else got rid of them by sending them to the central camp at Buchenwald.

TEN
THE AEROPLANES ARE COMING

FROM ROLAND'S MEMOIR

This was the fate of a decent peasant from my neighbourhood, innocent and gentle as a lamb. He had his nose broken following an incident that I must describe.

The bedtime signal, a whistle, had gone. My comrade had dozed off, ready for sleep, when he felt someone pulling off his blankets. He sat up abruptly and resisted the action of two antagonists. He tried to push them away. Realising that they were dealing with someone not very strong, the two thieves changed their attempt at theft into a fight to get the spoils of combat more quickly. It was a short struggle, and the few Frenchmen nearby were unable to help their fellow countryman. A punch was thrown into the shadows and landed on my poor friend's nose. Blood flowed. The two responsible sneaked off promptly because the noise had attracted the guards.

The beaten man's condition inspired a certain pity, because the *Blockführer* [cellblock boss] who had been alerted called an assembly immediately. Several shrill blows of the whistle woke us up. Ignorant of what had happened, we wondered what event caused this untimely wake-up call. When we had lined up in the usual formation, we saw the victim appear. Our unfortunate friend's misshapen, blood-stained face was difficult to recognise. Our three long rows parted at once so as to open up a pathway between them. Our comrade had to point out the guilty parties who, naturally, had not responded to the cellblock chief's order to step out from the rows. Unfortunately, dazed by the punch and too concerned about keeping hold of his blankets to see his enemies during the fight, he couldn't recognise his two assailants. After a speech, perhaps the only time the *Blockführer* ever seemed reasonable, we were able to go back to bed.

The next morning, I learnt the details of this appalling business. Two days later, my friend left for Buchenwald. Six months later, I read for myself the date of his death on his individual record.

•

We were paid for our work in the Eisenach factory. Depending on the job or the speciality, wages varied from 3 to 15 marks. The marks were special and printed expressly for the numerous different camps in Germany. The most important thing was that this money let us buy our cigarettes (when they were distributed – generally monthly), and also basic products which 'free' or 'liberated' populations might not particularly value. They were second-rate products, not especially edible. I remember a rather sour yellowish pumpkin purée which was being sold for one mark per bowl. Pumpkins were also offered to us in another form. They were cut into slices and preserved in a chemical acid and so of course, they were very sharp. I made do with tasting them. A few months later, there's no doubt that I would have devoured them with gusto.

We also had turnips and big black radishes to delight us. We crunched happily on these relatively fresh and tasty vegetables compared to our daily rations. Sometimes for 50 pfennigs we were generously offered cottage cheese, containing absolutely no fat. These supplies generally came along so infrequently that our meagre wages were never in danger of running out. The only supplies we looked forward to were the cigarettes and tobacco.

We quickly smoked the thirty or so cigarettes given out monthly despite imposing strict rationing on ourselves. By the end of the fortnight the vast majority of us were deprived of our precious herb. That was when the mercenary ones showed themselves. They had carefully saved their allocation, knowing that each day its value increased. Tobacco was in effect the perfect product for bartering. It was a currency that was worth its weight in gold in every exchange. You could swap it for bread, margarine, sausage, soup and so on. Once supplies ran out the cigarette attained the tremendous price of a civilian Deutsche mark.

I wasn't much of a smoker, although tobacco was like a drug in this situation, I tried hard to save half of my allowance to buy bread. I rarely succeeded, however. The frustrated smokers became incredibly ingenious in their feverish pursuit of the object of their desire. They turned their pockets inside out, eagerly sought out the guard for the honour of having his fag end. With several pinches of tobacco, some stale breadcrumbs, some dust, paper from an old cigarette butt, finally they managed to roll themselves a skinny cigarette which they revelled in. Personally, I didn't follow their example but I couldn't blame them. A comrade and I shared a pipe which he owned. I think this pipe is still carefully preserved, not in memory of times past, but as a sign of gratitude. It allowed us to make the most of this precious consolation right up to the last flake.

The general poverty warped our spirits and turned our thoughts towards theft. Young people among us, adolescents even, corrupted by several years of captivity, were devoid of all morality. They were ready to steal at the smallest opportunity. Their skill and cunning made them impossible to catch out. However, if they were caught red-handed the punishment was severe. The guilty man was beaten mercilessly by his own countrymen, the most vicious of whom was of course the victim of the theft.

This punishment was always violent but did not preclude the official penalty. Most of our 'officers' never resisted an opportunity to practise their kickboxing properly. The habit of these thieves was to deny the evidence. If one was caught in the act of breaking the lock on a cupboard after bedtime, he would state that in the darkness he had mistaken the cupboard, despite it being forbidden to be on that side at night and even though his own cupboard was 20 metres away. Unfortunately, most often it turned out that the offenders suffered no consequences and profited in peace from the fruits of their petty thefts. Suspicions were useless in the face of the outright and sometimes violent denials by the accused.

•

During this period, the air-raid warnings were quite frequent, but always took place in the daylight. It seemed to us that the siren was gloomier in the daytime. The team at work left their machines hurriedly, sometimes without turning them off, as did the conscripts and the Germans, even though it was against the rules. We assembled and the cheap labour was simply sent down into the basement of the building. The night shift, abruptly woken up from their sleep, also had to assemble and catch up with the day shift. This change of place did not involve any additional security measures but was greatly welcomed, at least by the day shift who had the advantage of a much-appreciated extra rest, in addition to the psychological satisfaction owed to these airborne visitors.

One day we found out that the factory adjacent to the central camp at Buchenwald had been completely demolished. Many victims were recorded, among them, unfortunately, many deportees and non-German workers. The same number of Germans had been killed as non-Germans. It was the only consolation for friends of the innocent victims. From then on, we left our basements and were led to the trenches that had been dug out around the barracks by civilian conscripts. Frightened by the air raid, they had scattered into the surrounding countryside – the only place of certain, if not complete, safety.

Summer had given way to autumn when we had the benefit of these still not very secure shelters. They were located within the enclosure of this vast factory of which we only took up about one-twentieth or one-thirtieth of the whole. In fact, it did not take long for intensive bombing to start. The warning had sounded about half an hour ago. We were in the trench covered with wooden beams, which were themselves overloaded with earth. We listened intently. We heard a muffled sound, which became clearer with the passing of each second, then the recognisable roar left us in no doubt about the imminent outcome. Indeed, explosions resounded more or less close together, more or less violent.

Under our shelters we were in complete darkness, with only the air vents letting in a glimmer of light; we stuck together, not through fear but through instinct. Suddenly the thunder seemed to crash down on us, the air vibrated in our ears. Several explosions very nearby deafened us. All of us crouched down, some of us were even trembling. For less than one or two minutes, an undeniable fear made us cower. Then the storm moved away. We appeared to have been the final target. A quarter of an hour later, the end of the air-raid warning sounded. We climbed out of our inadequate shelters. The spectacle that met our gaze was truly revelatory. Several bombs had fallen near us. Some of the huts were damaged. From the interior, enormous plumes of blackish smoke rose towards the sky, a sign of victory. Bravo, we thought, objective fulfilled. Our joy was even more deeply felt because we had emerged unharmed from the adventure. And of all the workers, we were the most exposed. Satisfied with the results, we turned our attention to the usual routine. Soup time had passed and our stomachs were letting us know. We were told that soup would be served on the spot and that immediately afterwards we would go to clear rubble. This confirmed, even if unwittingly, the effectiveness of the bombing.

Our block must also have been affected because we didn't go back to it once the air raid was over. Many were worried about their personal things, their meagre provisions etc., but innocently perhaps, I rejoiced in the knowledge that our captors were in an awkward position. Once we had swallowed our soup, several teams formed. We went to the most stricken areas. There, most of the buildings were blazing. Some of them had already collapsed. The iron beams were twisted, trees uprooted, the ground strewn with tiles, bricks, earth, scrap iron. Sometimes the cheerful fire pierced the black smoke with its sarcastic flames. It seemed to be laughing at the well-deserved disaster and welcomed us in a friendly way.

We were led there without being shouted at or beaten. It seemed as if our masters, who were arrogant yesterday, saw some kind of divine warning in this punishment. Our place of work was a building that was burning at one end with a distinctive sound. We had to recover various sets of aluminium alloy components before the fire took hold of them. We formed an assembly line to carry out our work which was frequently interrupted. Those who were inside rushed outside at the smallest strange sound, some going through the windows, others through the doors or fissures. Our guards didn't react to these precautions forced on us through legitimate fear and basic cautiousness. In any case, they too were feeling weak and in the grip of misfortune.

We soon got used to these various noises, the causes of which were unknown to us but which didn't result in anything. We still continued to feign fear and were able thus to reclaim some precious minutes for our feeble carcasses. Evening took us by surprise as we laboured. We were led back to our block. What would we find? There the damage was limited.

No bomb had fallen directly on the target. The violent blast had caused all the windows to break, the shrapnel had pierced the ceiling in several places. All of this brought home to us the fragility of these speedily erected buildings. Anyway, our accommodation remained habitable. After a quick distribution of the evening meal – the electricity had fallen victim to this memorable day – we went to bed. Several days were spent in clearing, filling in, collecting, shifting. Unfortunately, the electricity was restored quite quickly and we resumed our usual timetable. Its relatively slow pace was slowed down even more. The night shift was reduced to blessed unemployment for around ten days. The partially ripped curtains did not offer sufficient camouflage. Three weeks went by before the normal order of things resumed. Only the broken windows and the holes in the ceiling bore witness in our confined area to the destruction that had taken place. The disappearance of the glass windowpanes, which were impossible to replace and which it was judged pointless to repair, led subsequently to icy temperatures.

This second experience suffered by Eisenach was ample proof of the vulnerability of our trench-shelters. Once again, our masters bowed down to events and decided to adopt the only secure shelter: the countryside. We had to wait a week for the first air-raid warning that gave us the opportunity to take a country walk. Our blessed assailants no doubt thought that this period of time was essential to the restoring of the natives' spirits. It was true. I still remember the weather we were having during this dreaded second airborne expedition.

Autumn had put on its most beautiful finery. It had equipped itself with summer skies and spring temperatures. We had set ourselves up at the edge of a small wood next to a field of stubble which had been partially ploughed. Many people were moving along a road on the other side of this huge field. They too were getting away. The unmistakeable humming, muffled at first then becoming increasingly distinct, preceded the appearance of these messengers of freedom. They were flying very high up, leaving behind them a white trail which lasted for a long time in the sky. Little by little, this slim trail grew wider and paler then faded and disappeared. Metallic reflections glinted off the wings of the aircraft to wonderful effect. For us, they were glittering lures which we yearned to fly towards. To our great astonishment, they arrived from all sides. It seemed as if they had arranged to meet up directly above our heads. The bombing began of the town, the factory, of strategic points in the area such as road junctions. Sometimes we saw the bomb, we followed it with our eyes. As it hit the ground a black cloud arose immediately, followed by a muffled explosion to complete the performance. *Touché,* we all thought.

Our eyes were laughing even while our faces wore grave expressions or were deliberately unsmiling. We couldn't rejoice in front of our tyrants, who were worried and deep in thought.

The departure of our eventual liberators always left us with an impression of sadness. The happy moment in which we felt we were the conquerors of a tragic trap was coming to an end. Once again, we felt the heavy burden of our enslavement. We regrouped, then went to our different posts along the same path. This was the time when the bombings were escalating; whether during the day or at night they were always welcome.

Of course, we didn't go into the countryside at night. The usual supervision would not have been possible and despite the fear of punishment, we would have been tempted by the great adventure. Then the joy of our freedom would have been impossible to describe, given that it would have had the added taste of forbidden fruit. However, and fortunately, this devilish temptation was never offered to us.

During the night-time raids we went into a concrete shelter constructed on the ground floor of the neighbouring building parallel to ours. To get there, we went through the guardhouse adjoining the room with the toilets in our block, which gave onto a small terrace. From there, we got to the ground via a ramp rapidly installed for this use. We crossed the yard where, during the good old days, we sometimes used to breathe in the wholesome country air, and reached the shelter. It was composed of several rooms furnished with numerous benches. The necessary tools and accessories were there. It didn't take long for our workforce, varying between 400 and 450 men, to fill up the entire shelter. There was even a certain haste to get there first because stragglers found all the benches occupied and had to stand up. The short journey in the strong wind made us feel the icy temperature of the autumn nights. Sometimes our attention was caught by a beautiful starry sky, a rare sight in this gloomy country and one that we had forgotten.

The shelter where we were all squashed together did not take long to warm up. After twenty minutes the atmosphere was warmish and perhaps even a bit fetid. Then we dozed off and if the day shift in general hoped for a short air raid so they could go back to bed – still more comfortable despite everything – the night shift on the contrary wished for a protracted air raid. In any case, each one of us in both shifts found that these night raids went by very fast. I remember one particular night when the shift on the job and also the sleepers spent nine hours out of twelve in the shelter during the air raid. This was a record never achieved since. That time, as opposed to my usual luck, I was on the day shift. It goes without saying that there was a headcount each time we emerged from our walled enclosure and each time we returned to it. That's why the absolute rule was always to go through the doors two at a time, holding each other's arm. Furthermore, we had to be diligent and always be hard on the heels of those ahead of us. The slightest delay en route was sanctioned with a slap, always delivered with conviction.

Out of habit, it was second nature to us to think of these actions as intrinsic to the German character. Our only reaction was to think: 'Oh why can't I provoke him to single combat?' Then in the face of our inescapable powerlessness, we stomached it.

Our relationships with the French civilian workers, conscripts or volunteers, were the subject of controversy. In general, however, we weren't treated with all the compassion that our sad fate should have inspired. Fraternising with each other was forbidden and was not sought out for any charitable reason. We were the poor dispossessed and as such we offered no material advantage. Our fraternising would have been of no use to them.

•

I have a good memory of one single person, of the fairer sex, but a voluntary worker. Her selfless contribution of food helped me perhaps to stay alive. For three months, thanks to her, I had extra soup almost every day which was of great comfort to me. Sometimes she even gave me a brioche of white bread which seemed to me a delectable food, or her morning snack of brown bread and butter. I have never appreciated the delicious flavour of butter as much as on this occasion. And over the autumn after the air raids, this same person brought me fruit, pears or apples that she had pinched from trees in the countryside. I can accept that the soup she procured for me was surplus, but she still had to bother herself with a mess kit at the factory exit, in the refectory and in her room. Her actions were even more praiseworthy given that generally soup was exchanged for the monthly cigarette ration. Other kindnesses that I benefitted from were taken out of her own ration. Her work companion also made me a few gifts, but only when I went to *Kontrol* [the Head Office] where the two of them were employed. The latter had her husband on site which meant no doubt that she devoted all her bodily, physical and emotional attentions to him.

As for the workers themselves, in my opinion and in the opinion of those I associated with, they behaved towards us in a squalid fashion.

Two examples, from among a thousand, will prove it. Autumn brought with it cold snaps. Our light-weight uniform was ineffective protection against the prevailing temperature. I therefore expressed the wish to exchange tobacco for a pullover. I soon found a purchaser through the intermediary of a deported comrade. Consent was granted for the exchange of a part wool, part cotton pullover for a packet of twenty cigarettes and a 50gm packet of tobacco, along with the promise of a second packet of cigarettes at the next distribution.

You would have to have lived our misery, you would have to have known the priceless value of our tobacco to understand the inequality, the immorality, the greed of this swap. The civilian, an ex-prisoner, had not deprived himself of an invaluable product. He had lived through many German winters; he knew how to distinguish between the useful and the superfluous. Nevertheless, he agreed this deal and carried it out, not thinking of the value that he himself attributed to this sweater but judging the value that I attributed to it.

This exchange would only have been carried out by one in ten of us because tobacco was so highly prized. Today, with the benefit of hindsight, I despise such behaviour even more. And I have all the more gratitude towards a prisoner of war whose *Kommando* was tasked with mitigating the damage caused by the bombing. After the catastrophe at Eisenach, this *Kommando* was sent to us. The French prisoners who had been suffering mental distress for over four years easily sensed our physical depression and our brutalisation. One of them on his own initiative gave me a small cotton summer shirt without showing the least desire for some kind of compensation. I would have offered it to him in vain, I am sure. How many other deportees successfully scrounged either a few cigarettes or a bit of tobacco? Whereas I have no memory of having heard about a deportee getting the necessary from a free worker to roll a skinny cigarette. The opposite occurred more frequently.

The second example is more succinct, but no less relevant. In this autumn season, the military operations seemed crucial to us every day. The slightest gain in territory reported by the German newspapers to us was a sign of undeniable victory. Every morning we asked for news of the war as soon as we made contact with the civilians; generally, however, we only received quite vague answers. One day, I put several questions about this to a scrawny man with a broom whose sole task was to ensure the cleanliness – completely relative – of a section of this huge workshop. He stopped whistling, stopped sweeping and answered: 'Oh, as for me, you know…' In the sense that beyond his broom, his soup, his bed and no doubt his whistling, he didn't care about anything. Did he think his fate was tolerable? I don't know, but he certainly knew how to adapt to it.

Pathetic fellow. Perhaps now that the broom handle no longer feeds you, you miss your enchanted stay in Eisenach? It is difficult to wield a big handle skilfully, whether it be a broom, a pickaxe or a shovel, when you are bone idle. His answer really struck me; I still remember it. That's why I do not agree with the 'deportees', whom I would designate as voluntary workers, being able to enjoy privileges concurrently with the prisoners of war and us. A deportee is someone who is transported under armed escort on the alert, not someone who takes the tourist passenger train.

•

Now the autumn spread its veil of sorrow over the already bleak countryside. The frequent rains kept the ground permanently wet. The cold spells, thankfully slowly, made the surrounding air very chilly, an atmosphere that we were not used to. Work became a painful grind. Not properly dressed, underfed, we were left defenceless against the inclement weather, even though it was not yet harsh. The daytime air raids caused us an overload of physical suffering compensated by the emotional satisfaction that, at the same time, they never failed to inspire. The dayshift leading the way went in the direction of the countryside. Many times, the fine rain, the cold wind, the dismal weather gave us a foretaste of the threatening winter to come. We slid along waterlogged ground on our badly shod feet. They soon mingled with the greyish earth. However, the double-quick pace that we were obliged to keep up – the stragglers at any rate – warmed us up a bit. The run wasn't very long, about a kilometre, and was over irregular ground which forced us frequently to make physical efforts to maintain or restore our shaky balance.

Then we reached our objective. This wasn't the edge of the wood anymore but the middle of a huge field where a row of trees hid us – perhaps from those who weren't even looking for us. There we collected together, clinging to each other to mitigate the grip of the wind. A few made use of the protection of a hollow tree trunk. All these precautions were pointless. The wind everywhere always managed to find us. We shivered stoically. The cloudy sky hid from us the comforting sight of multiple airborne squadrons. Only the sound told us these bringers of justice were passing over our heads. Sometimes we heard a swift hellish roaring right next to us, but we still couldn't see anything. These flyovers across Germany were not without danger. The Allied air force losses were certainly quite substantial. On several occasions, we had the opportunity to be present at the swaying, elegant descent of parachutists whose plane had been shot down without us even realising.

We assumed that the plane had been brought down by the anti-aircraft defences which offered the only defence of the area. There was no Nazi fighter command. The few fighters available in the region were probably for propaganda purposes. They took off when the air-raid warning sounded but remained invisible during the bombing. The appearance of the parachutes in particular attracted our attention. We knew they were our friends and their misfortune tugged at our hearts. We would have liked to see them fall by our sides so that we could question them, look at them, see in them what we had once been – strong, healthy, vigorous men. Despite the force of habit, we were aware of our physical debility, our flagging moral standards, our decaying dignity. The sight of a free human being fighting for an ideal reinvigorated us. Our faith was energised, boosted. He was still far away, this free man, but our imaginations filled in what we could not see. Sometimes too, we escaped from this degrading atmosphere of subjugation, of enslavement. During these precious moments with our thoughts full of a serene and exhilarating idea, we forgot about the rigours of the weather. In these moments of bliss, our wet, frozen feet and our shivering bodies could not bring us back to the gloomy reality. But the raucous shouts, the brutal interjections of the mastiffs guarding us – and I'm insulting dogs here – were stronger than our own sufferings and came to break the reverie.

Sometimes a cloud of smoke rose on the earth's horizon. This could only be a downed plane which was burning. Once, we even saw a seat fall nearby. We were able to examine it. Its shape, its construction showed deficient manufacturing which made us sure of its nationality. It was probably a fighter who had gone astray and who had been reduced to pieces by a flying fortress. What a pleasure it would have been for us if the plane had come down. Its combustion would have had the effect of a joyful bonfire announcing a better future. Its sizzling would have been celestial music. The fumes themselves would have been intoxicating perfumes.

During this time, accustomed to the total inhumanity of our hosts, we felt in return a crazy, incomprehensible, absolute hatred towards them. There could be no spectacle that they were victims of that could move us. No atrocity done to them could be either unjustified or unlawful. Blood calls for blood, crime desires crime, savagery claims savagery. Nowadays, some people feel sorry for them, those who have never known either what it is to be a true prisoner of war or the Nazi camps. That vile, abject, despicable person who holds on to a constant tenacious rancour towards his neighbour down the hall but who forgets how comprehensively France was violated.

Aside from the emotional satisfaction, these brief forays into the country also brought us material advantages, at least for the most foolhardy. We crossed various fields. The stubble offered a few heads of wheat or rye, whose hard, greyish seeds we chewed whole. However, this permitted harvest wasn't very fruitful. The field had been raked and the heads gleaned. The birds had been able to perfect this work over several months; we provided the finishing touches and these were few and far between, especially since we did not slow our pace.

Sometimes another path led us to the same end. A field of beetroot offered itself to our appetites. Our path met this field at an acute angle. Right from the start, unbeknownst to the guards, the most fearless among us nimbly swerved and grabbed a beetroot from the spongy ground; sometimes the earth held on tightly to its fruit and only the leaves remained in the bold one's hand, leaving him crestfallen. In all these cases, the example was contagious. The stripped corner grew bigger each time we crossed it, despite the attention aroused in our guards. When we left this sympathetic field, the corner was bare along a middle portion of 20 metres. Personally, I was never reduced to eating this vegetable, not because of a lack of appetite or contempt, but perhaps because of a sense of my dignity. I still strove to differentiate myself from an animal.

These days, I acknowledge that the few beetroots I could have stolen might have usefully improved my pitiful daily ration. Ultimately, a field of recently harvested potatoes had more success. This field was vast and the harvesting had been done mechanically. Many potatoes had been forgotten, for a short while at least. A peasant was there in his field as we passed. Oblivious of this civilian, and probably attracted by the beautiful bait, the least docile among us or the most starving threw themselves onto this fertile earth and as fast as they could, collected up as many as their tireless bony hands could hold. However, the peasant was not indifferent as he witnessed this quite natural reaction on our part. Armed with a cudgel he ran towards us and hit out randomly. The benefit was too unexpected for us to abandon it before our supply was complete.

On that particular day I couldn't resist such a tempting show. I went all over the place with maximum speed picking up these windfall root vegetables. All of a sudden, I found myself next to this peasant whom I had thought harmless. But the thwack of a stick on my bent spine delivered with all the heart and enthusiasm worthy of the most ardent Nazi made me realise that I had collected enough. I had paid heavily for them. That day, I also understood that neutrality – I won't say sympathy – towards the German must never be sought, first of all out of respect for our dignity, and then for our security. The German is anti-French, let us be even more anti-German. Let us strive for hatred, for despite all our efforts the hatred we inspire will always be stronger, more tenacious, than that which we feel.

However, to prove that I am not speaking because of resentment, or even rancour, I must acknowledge that I met one German, only one, who was sympathetic and human. On one single occasion, I was the object of completely unprecedented attention from our often-furious *Blockführer* that

I must depict. Of medium height, quite athletic, he knew how to look the part of the boss. At the many daily gatherings, his arrival customarily signalled standing to attention followed by a *Mützen ab* [caps off]. Once the door was closed again, he would stop, draw himself up and consider the line-up with a long gaze. Then he would go along our interminable line, three rows deep, his chest puffed out, clicking his heels on the ground, just like a real general reviewing his troops. He would return at the same pace. Satisfied with having demonstrated his impeccable style, he inspected the staff. Then it was stand at ease, *Mutzen auf* [caps on] and the return to work. That was the physical behaviour. The mental behaviour stemmed from this. An unparalleled brutality characterised our chief. He was present at any opportunity to hit someone. He never shied away from such occasions and worked with admirable enthusiasm.

When he had to wait too long for his favourite task, he knew how to create confusion among us which required his authority urgently. The air-raid warnings offered the key opportunity. Once the siren went off, the resting shift rushed towards the exit, not exactly out of fear from the danger, but to get a seat in the cellblock because by then winter had arrived and we had left the countryside. After a few minutes there was a shapeless, messy, fluctuating crowd in front of the door. With each passing second, the crowd grew bigger. Our little *Führer* was there. With a mocking eye, he observed this mess, as we elbowed each other. Then his smile changed and suddenly he leapt towards this brutalised mass of body parts with his feet and fists flying. His always unforeseen arrival caused a hasty retreat. His blows were fierce with nothing to mitigate them.

He stopped, out of breath. The group had taken shape and formed a line, making an orderly exit possible. The doorway – a simple door – was narrow. The rush towards the door, the pushing, had in the past created 'caged areas' and as a result some slowing down of the block's evacuation. Our *Führer* had quickly sorted out this mess. His violent interventions meant that speed of execution had replaced haste. Any vague move on our part was severely punished. In these circumstances with the blows being predictable, the French wisely stayed at the back. They awaited their turn patiently and thus avoided a mean punishment, doubtless slightly justifiable, but oh ever so slightly.

Personally, when the sirens startled me in bed, I waited for as long as possible before getting out of a warm bunk – uncomfortable of course, but in the circumstances really comfortable. But this contempt for potential danger was no longer allowed. Our man realised after the first rush that, indeed, there was a slowdown in the flow of sleepers. He guessed the reason. What a superb occasion to exhibit his rage. Whip at the ready, he made his way along the rows of bunks and struck the men with all his strength, with all his exacerbated hatred. I was situated quite far from the entrance so I could see the danger approaching. This time the real threat was in view. Hastily, I rose, got dressed. I needed less than a minute. Usually I left just in time. However, one night my vigilance was caught out. I was not sufficiently fast and I couldn't leave my sector before the critical moment. A crack of the whip at leg height caught me as I fled.

Other impulses to hit encouraged this depraved individual, this vicious sadist. Sundays were primarily devoted to chores. Everyone used this weekly day of rest to good effect: sleeping, washing, mending, haircuts etc.... and the last few hours of leisure were devoted to reading or games, such as cards, chess, draughts etc... When we became aware of the whistle and the demand for ten, fifteen or twenty volunteers, each one of us innocently moved away from the danger zone and the demand went unanswered.

Stunned at such a result and completely incapable of suspecting the reasons for it, our officer repeated his demand more vehemently. Same lack of success. Then he realised that this misconduct, this disobedience constituted a humiliation for him, a serious act of insolence towards him. His reaction was immediate. He chased those who were now running away, kicking and punching all the while. A few groups who couldn't get away and who had stayed where they were impassively, untroubled even, suffered a brutal assault when called. Only shortness of breath put an end to this fury.

And yet the punishment was not enough. Such a humiliation deserved collective reprisals.

Several sharp blasts of the whistle, hateful commands of *'Aufstehen'* [stand up] called for us to assemble. Immediate obedience prevailed. We had to stand still for a half-hour to mark the occasion. The chore was chosen at random. Then release and... waiting...

As paradoxical as it sounds, one day I inspired pity in this stone of a man. It was in autumn, and we were coming back from a long air raid. I was moving along painfully in my inadequate footwear. Little by little I had fallen back to the tail end of the column. We were about 100 metres from the finish. The ground along this pathway was as slippery as an ice rink. My wooden soles which were missing the worn-out heels made me walk slowly and carefully in order to avoid falling. The Krauts who brought up the rear harassed me or taunted me with insults. Faced with my good will and especially in view of my obvious helplessness they didn't hit me but left me to the rear-guard soldier, the last bastion.

In spite of my efforts to avoid the contact I feared, someone quickly caught up with me. I had anticipated a couple of slaps and prepared myself to bear it stoically when I felt someone take my arm and lead me in a friendly way to help me walk. Yet my immediate reaction was to try to hurry up. Then, the fury of the previous evening said to me, in an unexpectedly calm and serene voice: *'pomalo',* a Russian word whose meaning I knew, 'gently'. And so I arrived late yet unpunished. My one-time benefactor told me to get my shoes repaired by the cellblock's cobbler [*Schumacher*] and he exempted me from a few hours of work following the air raid.

I made the most of it by washing my shoes and my feet and by going for a lie-down. I told a good comrade about this gesture and like me, he was completely astounded. I had been taken for a Russian but I don't think that if my nationality had been known it would have stopped this unusual compassion in our environment. We couldn't inspire more hatred, nor more fear than the red Russian, as far as I know. The intention was therefore even more praiseworthy and more inconceivable since it concerned a Russian.

These air raids gave rise to frequent clothes washing. Each time we went out in bad weather, my socks – made from old rags and strips of material – were wet through and muddy when we came back. We had to rinse them through several times in plenty of running water. In these cold temperatures, we dreaded this job; yet it had to be done as a precautionary measure. Drying times were long. On Sundays, we took advantage of the piped hot water to speed things up. However, my reserves were not enough to provide for the inevitable necessities.

I was obliged to adopt the only effective method: at each air-raid warning I quickly removed the thick envelope of mismatched and poorly attached cloths from my feet. Then, with my feet on my wooden soles, I set off courageously into the mud, the water, the cold. I felt some satisfaction at having removed the need for such a miserable duty. When the mud transformed the walk into a slide, I soon found myself barefoot. I picked up my decrepit clogs and went on my way. This was how I managed to avoid being left behind and being the object of vigilance which I didn't like.

I think this is when the pre-bestial period we were enduring ended. Winter ushered in a new era; an era of bestiality.

ELEVEN
THE ERA OF BESTIALITY

FROM ROLAND'S MEMOIR

Germany was newly surrounded and could no longer hope for economic support from subjugated nations. Replenishing supplies became a problem, a crisis. The civil populations bore the first repercussions, which then became worse as they passed to the voluntary or forced labourers, then to the prisoners of war and finally reached their fullest extent when they arrived at the last layer – ours, the deportees.

Our portions were cut each week. First of all, the daily bread ration, which varied according to the day but was always a minimum of 500gm, was brought back to a consistent 500gm. This amount was cut to 450, 400, then down to 350gm. This might seem sufficient to the novice. To anyone who knows the density and nutritional inadequacy of German black bread, it will seem pathetic. Then the soups became insipid, the canteen allowances diminished, tobacco distribution became less frequent. The few nutritious foods disappeared from our menu, such as jam and honey – which were substitutes for the real thing anyway.

Then the inadequate supplies that the free workers obtained for us became less and less frequent, then disappeared completely following a reduction in vouchers and food rations. Within the space of a month, our food ration had shrunk by a third, the following month it had shrunk by a half. Another reason for the lack of food was the cold. Winter had us in its icy grip.

The superficial damage caused by the bombing was still only in the process of being repaired. The window panes were replaced with planks. This meant we could observe the huge size of these broad panels. Installing them involved considerable acrobatics. The prisoners of war who had to carry out this work, aware of the purpose of the bombing, dawdled and skived off. It was freezing inside the factory. Each man at his post sought shelter, but the freezing air infiltrated everywhere.

An electric washing machine ran during the day close to the inspection area. There were some perforated pipes situated in the upper section at the front which poured a whitish caustic soda-based liquid onto oily, dirty components placed beneath. Once cleaned up, the parts passed to the back. There, a warm air autoclave dried them rapidly. This autoclave was fitted with quite a broad flange and had a sliding door that closed vertically.

We coveted this place all the time, this 'bench' with a heated backrest. I was well placed to observe the surrounding area and as soon as an opportune moment presented itself, I slid deftly towards the autoclave. I was often beaten to it by one or two of the other deportees, but the improvised bench offered three seats. Those who were seated on either side kept watch while the third man succumbed to bliss. When danger approached from one side, we left our heated spot from the opposite side. We pretended to busy ourselves with crates of components waiting to be cleaned or shipped. But it was rare that we fooled anyone. When the danger of being beaten up was imminent we dashed off as quickly as we could into the maze of machine aisles and dividing walls. Then we returned furtively to our places.

Another place that we also often visited were the toilets. They were in a small room with only one window. Our frequent visits warmed it up little by little. The cigarette stubs that we smoked there helped with the heating. When the air warmed up, the attendance, the frequent comings and goings aroused the attention of the guards. One of them was quick to make an abrupt and brutal entrance which caused disruption and provoked a general stampede.

The unfortunate person caught out red-handed smoking was victim of a punishment. A few hours later, there was the same recurrence of mad panic in the same place for the same reasons. The night shift behaved in the same way and had the same worries.

The washing machine benefitted from a conducive semi-darkness. The furnace was turned on, luckily it was silent, and the aficionados arrived one by one. Keeping a look-out was still essential. Rapid retreats were helped by the voluntarily very low lighting. The main thing in all these circumstances of collective laziness was not to be grabbed by an angry fist. Sometimes I received a stray slap or a random kick, but I always managed to slip away adroitly.

To protect ourselves from the cold we used one of the two blankets that we had, usually the smallest. We wrapped it around our upper bodies as well as we could and tried to make our improvised attire look inconspicuous. Our trick was discovered. The order was given not to wrap ourselves in blankets – which we believed, and I mention it in my defence if it's true – was to prevent us from exchanging them for food. A few complied, most ignored it. The order was given again without any noticeable result. Then it seemed as if this incident was forgotten. A week went by.

Just like every morning we were dressed in this shapeless woollen fabric. We had arrived at our respective posts where, significantly less chilly, we sought to kill time, when suddenly a rumour reached us: the *Blockführer* was going around the factory checking clothing. At the inspection post located at the opposite end of our block, we would have been able to get to the toilets and take off our blankets. A companion suggested this solution to me. I didn't accept this. I didn't believe that this single means of protecting ourselves from the cold could result in punishment. Despite my great experience, on this occasion I was gullible. So we waited. The *Blockführer* appeared, came up to me, asked me the question while feeling me. I answered *'Ja'*. I received a couple of slaps in the face, arms by my side. He took down my army number. This was a way of avoiding triggering a more violent reaction. When you were caught red-handed, no hope of a successful escape, you had to confront the danger defiantly. A couple of slaps in the face were usually the opening move that provoked some instinctive gesture of self-defence in the victim. This gesture annoyed the brute who redoubled his attack. At the same time the victim of the assault tried harder to protect himself from the killer punches. Ultimately, the beating was severe, ending in a trickle of pale red blood as a result of this unfair battle of the strong versus the weak. You had to master your fear and repress your instincts. This doesn't mean I despise such behaviour any less.

Numb with cold, weakened through hunger, despairing of ever seeing the end of such suffering one day, our minds would wander off. The routine of unchanging horizons blighted our imagination. Our feelings towards our families seemed to have melted away at the same time as our bodies. We rarely elevated our thoughts towards loved ones or beloved places. Our sentimentality was abolished… we had to live. Our conversations generally centred around food. What succulent dishes were conjured up in these starving places! What details, what vocabulary in the preparation of culinary masterpieces! These chats seemed to me misplaced and uncalled-for. The imagination on this topic had expanded out of all proportion. And the height of innocence itself in my opinion was to note down recipes. How many men carefully wrote down on some piece of paper how to make such special dishes. How many men against all rational thinking took down addresses, promised they would visit each other in turn? How many of those men will never see each other again?

From this date on, my forward thinking was concentrated all the time on this latter subject. In comparison with my poor comrades I only engaged in a few projects. And if I did, I knew in advance that they were very unpredictable. And yet I wasn't sceptical about my fate, nor was I demoralised in regard to my predictions. However, I had lost the marvellous optimism that had kept me hoping over the first six months for our deliverance at an early date. Once this date was reached, I postponed it for a bit, and thus it continued for several months. Then winter came, our suffering increased, the progressive weakening of our bodies brought us lower little by little. Our prison for us was what the barn is for the beast: the place where you eat, where you sleep. There was no longer anything that could arouse a human reflex or feeling. There we took our first steps into the realm of the animals. A few months later, we were to find ourselves right in the midst of it.

During this time, I had become friends with a Parisian man whose deportation had been preceded by quite a long period of imprisonment in Fresnes. In prison his physical resistance had been severely sapped. In Eisenach he contracted jaundice and the only remedy, a prolonged diet, weakened him considerably. We were very similar. Brotherhood in suffering is impossible and yet that happened to us. We shared our sorrows and found them less bitter. When we were part of the same night or day shift, we slept in the same bunk even though some bunks weren't occupied. This meant we had four blankets on top of us and we warmed each other up. It was the only way to feel the benevolent effects of the warmth. Sometimes we were solitary.

After work, the day shift could still warm themselves up a bit or sleep in spite of the cold. The night shift on the other hand was compelled to sleep in the daytime and slept very badly after twelve hours without sleep.

I will never forget my returns to the block at six in the morning. I arrived literally freezing but nevertheless happy not to be attached to a work bench anymore. Our only comfort was a tepid coffee. The most careful among us had kept back a piece of bread from the day before and ate it slowly. Others – I was always among them – drank the ersatz drink if it was hot and launched themselves onto their respective straw mattresses. Personally, I always took great care to tuck my blankets in tightly. I spread out my few rags up to my chest as well as I could. I placed my precious socks under my flattened bolster to avoid theft and put my shoes under the mattress at the foot of the bunk to avoid either theft, pure and simple, or exchange. It was a precaution, however, that I didn't have to take frequently, unfortunately. My shoes weren't going to attract attention.

Finally, wearing only underpants, bare-chested and shirt in hand, I went over to a lighted area. There I inspected my shirt and always killed a few fleas. Then I put it back on, not on account of decency, and inspected my underpants, then once again fully covered I slid gently into bed. There the cold made itself oddly felt, especially on the legs. I curled up the best I could, rubbed the soles of my frozen feet with scrawny hands. I tried to use all of my own heat, keeping my head under the blankets; finally, with a supreme effort, in a supreme test, I flapped my legs with short quick movements. Exhaustion and weakness prevented me from exercising like this. I soon ran out of breath and stopped, realising the pointlessness of any efforts. I waited for sleep to prevail over temperature. That didn't take long in fact and generally I was asleep by around seven or seven-thirty. But what a short sleep! At ten-thirty or eleven at the latest I woke up with my legs as cold as ever. The light, the noise made by the *Stubendienst* [cleaning detail] cleaning up and especially the hopelessness of getting a second sleep imposed a painful wait on me.

At midday, the shift on duty came back to swallow the daily soup. From my bed I watched jealously as they ate this rapid, meagre meal. Then

I got up after their return to work. The wait was so long… I had to spend several hours on an empty belly doing nothing.

Luckily, I was an animal. I went here and there poking around aimlessly, observing without seeing. At 17:00 hours, the command *Aufstehen* [get up] officially sanctioned what was already a *fait accompli*. Finally, the moment of our double meal was near. I had been present as the loaves of bread were put out to share around the table, I had concerned myself with the food on offer. Despite myself, I had constantly stimulated my appetite – unfortunately, never to the point of reducing it. Finally, the soup that our comrades had been given at midday was distributed, followed immediately by the evening meal – bread and margarine or sausage. We swallowed everything too quickly, for words are wasted on a starving man. In our case hunger had become an instinct that sought constantly to satisfy itself. When the occasion arose once every twenty-four hours, we didn't lap up our soup but devoured it as ravenously as a starving dog. Then, unsatisfied but nevertheless slightly calmer, we got ready to face the onslaught of the freezing cold for the next twelve hours.

The ills that befell us were numerous and never arrived on their own. The conditions we lived in varied but had one identical characteristic: a moral stench.

The extreme cold had caused the water pipes to freeze. The overflowing toilets became unusable. They were replaced with two barrels with the bottoms taken out. These were placed between two shared wash basins which lent us support and made these unexpected latrines practicable.

It was at this time that a soup made from beetroot leaves caused light but widespread dysentery. The boss was consulted and advised not eating this soup as a cure. Unfortunately, hunger did not accept any deviation from its meagre diet. Notwithstanding the seriousness of acute dysentery in these places, most of the men couldn't accept leaving half of the daily meal without any substitute. In spite of abdominal pains followed by a mad dash to the lavatory, I myself could not control my hunger. After a fortnight of this vegetarian diet, the ordinary soup came back, no doubt because the stock of beetroot leaves ran out. It certainly wasn't any more or less nutritious, but it didn't cause illness. The dysentery left as it had arrived.

The day shift could fulfil this physiological need outside. Some pits had been dug for this purpose outside our building in the yard where we went sometimes on fine days for a breath of air. This meant there was always a keen crowd, some in a hurry, some not, gathered around the exit. When the crowd grew quite large, about ten men, a Kraut who was in charge of the shift supervised the session. There again it was a fight against time. The last ones were harassed and couldn't complete their needs in a decent fashion.

This perspective of progressive starvation made almost all of us slaves to our negligible private supplies. Each of us forced himself to keep back a fraction of his bread portion, fearing, quite justifiably, potential restrictions the next day. When there was a theft, what pain, what remorse, what rage it caused in the victim.

A few of us, two or three out of forty Frenchmen, still had a few tasty leftovers from a family parcel. How sparingly they helped themselves. I was indeed astonished to see these precautions. Were they really useful? I still wonder about that. Even more so because this display, as meagre as it was, could only arouse the attention of fellow countrymen using the same cupboard.

And in fact, a pot of jam, three-quarters empty, was suddenly found completely empty. The owner, a strapping lad, still quite robust compared to us, had his suspicions. It wasn't enough, but they were confirmed by the claims of certain others among his comrades. The alleged guilty party was questioned and denied it like the rest of his kind. He received a deserved punishment, even though he was French, which the victim meted out to him on his own without help from anyone else. We derived no pleasure from beating or seeing someone beaten.

•

We plunged into winter. Our cellblock had become damp. Our roughly constructed roof had been cracked by the last bombing and water seeped through in several places. On several occasions, there had been no warnings for the increasingly frequent air raids, which had prompted a slight panic, somewhat simulated by us, but real enough among our guards.

In any case, since then new precautions had been agreed upon much to our great joy. As soon as the *Voralarm* [prior alert] was announced during the night only, the shift on duty returned to the block. They had to wait there in silence, either for the warning itself or for the removal of danger. We were always happy to get back to our pigsty. While the air there was foul, it was still less freezing than in the factory. Moreover, a warm air vent sometimes worked at half capacity and its tepid breath made us huddle together tightly in a silent crush. It was a mass of people indifferent to the overcrowded conditions. Livestock don't have a sense of propriety; they don't know the rule of hygiene. Those who couldn't get into the slightly warmed area sought refuge in the washroom and toilets. This small space soon warmed up once it was filled with fifty or sixty human units. Unfortunately, when at last we were all feeling somewhat drowsy, a sudden sharp whistle alerted us to the end of the warning.

The cold didn't bother the lice. They reappeared in force after having disappeared for two months. In the face of this danger from the invaders, new hygiene measures were put in place. Less thorough than the first ones, they could only achieve less accurate results. Every Sunday morning to our great displeasure we underwent a lice inspection. We stripped off where we assembled, made a pile of our rags and completely naked, we passed in front of the nurse or his assistant. Then we went into the wash basin area where we had to wash ourselves down from top to toe with icy water, no soap and no towel. On these occasions I got as little water on me as possible. Then we got dressed again. Those who had lice were compelled to undergo a supervised wash and were given clean underwear. These sessions proved to me that we had adapted perfectly to freezing temperatures. In effect, stripped bare, we didn't shiver, we felt no colder than we did with clothes on.

Our reaction was the same; we held our elbows against our bodies, our shoulders hunched around our necks. When we put our clothes on again, we didn't feel any better. It seemed that from now on the cold was part of us. Only bodily contact with icy water prompted a sensation of cold, however real, followed afterwards by an impression of warmth, however false. Those who could still distinguish this difference were the fortunate ones. Whether through illness or lack of strength, some men no longer reacted to any contact, physical or emotional.

One day we had a small reinforcement where we came across six fellow countrymen, I think. We welcomed them as best we could and offered them a portion of our recently received cigarette ration. One of them in fact did not smoke. He still accepted our gift which he would be able to exchange. This acceptance upset a lot of people. They thought he shouldn't accept a share of something that he wasn't going to benefit from himself. This small detail shows how pernickety our generosity was. And several among us actually refused this act of mutual help. This was a really contemptible selfishness, because two or three cigarettes out of thirty were not going to leave an irredeemable void.

One of these six Frenchmen who was particularly emaciated was admitted to the sanatorium. The doctor there realised that he was dirty, lousy and suffering from dysentery. He told him to go and wash himself in the washroom nearby. His weakness was such that the unfortunate man soon returned just as filthy. A nurse was instructed to proceed with cleaning him up. He made him climb into the semi-cyclindrical basin, about 2 metres in length, and sit under a tap. He turned on the cold water. Three years on, I still see the poor man, skeletal, squatting on his haunches, hollow-chested, seeming not to feel the icy shower. I doubt these first ministrations helped to save a life already at risk.

Around this time my professional partner was a Russian, about thirty years old. We managed to communicate after a fashion in scrambled German. He told me that he was married, a father and that he was an engineer with the railways. He also told me that he contracted an illness the name of which I have forgotten. He was admitted to the sickbay then sent to Buchenwald. Some time later I had news of him from one of his fellow countrymen. He was dead. How many more have died whom I have forgotten?

News of the war came to us late or partly distorted and sometimes provoked in us surges of optimism.

But the days, the weeks, the months passed. We could never see an end in sight. Too many hopes had been dashed to allow us to continue hanging onto a scintilla of hope. And isn't hope life itself, the life of the soul? And what remained of this for us? Nothing.

Patiently we accomplished our daily drudgery, patiently we made the most of our free time to sleep, patiently we endured the beatings, the bad weather. We had become a real herd of livestock; we had the same reactions. The moments of panic when faced with the threat of the stick, the double-quick return to the barn, those muted silent struggles to get to the sheltered spot, that passive instinctive obedience to the same old orders. That lack of modesty, that indifference towards undressing in front of each other every day. That anxious wait for soup. We behaved like animals, nothing but animals. That was the work of six months of famine.

Even the idea of death faded in our imaginations. We no longer tensed at the thought of it in the ordinary human way. We realised that we would also have to deal with death if it occurred suddenly.

How many of us, utterly exhausted, understood our impending death in any case? A few, certainly. I had come to the conclusion that the moment of my death could come any day. I had become accustomed to thinking that my life was hanging by a thread and I never rebelled.

•

The year was coming to its end. We had hoped for a long time that this festival would bring a noticeable improvement in our everyday life. Then we were supposed to have three days of rest. This prolonged inactivity was mandated by the legal closure of the factory at Christmas. The few German civilians who worked with us obtained this favour for us without, of course, realising it. We had previously made up the two non-statutory days of rest by working the two preceding Sundays. The favour was therefore repaid.

The 25th December arrived. Our cellblock chiefs, three of them, with the help of a few Kraut prisoners, had put up a Christmas tree in front of the barred window – a real fir tree decorated with gold and silver ribbons. This sight against a snowy background would have been truly meaningful if the equally evocative bars had not been put there. In any case, a perfect scene would probably have left us indifferent. This one, incomplete and strange, did not stop us devoting all our thoughts to our usual subjects: a better meal no doubt and possible rest. A few vague memories of the Christmases of old were the only memories of the past.

Animals certainly have memories but so much shallower! The midday meal was not better in any way. As soon as I had finished, I went to lie down like most of the others. The evening soon arrived. Our last hope was finally going to be confirmed or quashed. We had to wait for the evening meal. That's a good omen, we thought. Bottles arrived, but filled with juice, then several barrels. They contained the extra food: potato salad.

Finally, barrels of beer which were sold in the canteen dating from two months ago.

This grim Christmas was no cause for celebration, neither in the material nor in the spiritual domain. Yet we appreciated the extra rest, the extra potatoes, however pathetic that seems.

New Year's Day was a Sunday like so many others. I was getting desperate to know how much longer our enslavement would last. I decided to believe that 100 days separated us from freedom. I confided my new and *nth* forecast to my comrade, at that time we were inseparable, adding that I didn't attribute any more value to this forecast than to the ones before, aware of my past failures.

That also added a thought to our infrequent thoughts. And often after our brief morning greetings I said to him, with a disillusioned and sceptical smile playing about my lips, 'another ninety-five, ninety or eighty days.' If we had both known that on the 102nd day we would be alive and free, with what bravery and with what spirit we would have borne the most critical period of our deportation. The output from our section was less and less significant. The indispensable raw materials such as copper, aluminium and tin were in short supply. The machines were working at half speed and only those fed with steel. At the inspection post, we checked the same components several times over. The factory seemed to be disintegrating. The night shift was frequently reduced by a good third. The happy beneficiaries returned to the cellblock smiling broadly. Germany was dying, but unfortunately, so were we. Happy were those who were tougher than Germany.

The Allied advance was continuing. Huge strides made were followed by long breaks. Fortunately for us, over the past few months we were no longer capable of reacting. After a few early warnings, it was decided to evacuate us. The scaffolding was taken down. The planks that made up the bunk frames were collected up and put into piles. The same with the straw mattresses. There was thick dust everywhere. We spent our last night in an unimaginable hovel. The next day after an unexpected morning soup and the allocation of a day's supplies, we returned our mess kits. And the convoy was organised. For the last time we crossed this hall where we had suffered so much, barely aware of it by the end. I don't believe there were any regrets because we didn't think we would find a skimpier diet than the one we were leaving behind, nor an icier atmosphere than the one in which we had been suffering. A last goodbye glance at the rare civilians who had shown compassion and pity towards our plight. I think they understood it better than us.

We went down this huge hill on whose summit the BMW factory had been built, for the fourth or fifth, indeed for the last time.

We walked along a broad road, along other smaller paths, and reached Eisenach station. A train was waiting for us. We were dispatched along the length of the train and waited, I suppose, for a free track. It was a fine day. A pale sun at this still early hour seemed to dwell on the fate that awaited us. It cast its brightest, warmest rays on this pack of men, food for a future bloodbath. The world over which it had just shone had not revealed a show of such cruelty, a drama whose end was so tragic. And yet, carefree from this moment, we were peacefully enjoying the delicious warmth thanks to the walking and the mildness of the weather.

An hour had passed when suddenly the air-raid warning sounded. As always, we welcomed it but it sent our guards into a frenzy of activity and we suffered the backlash. It meant we had to evacuate the station at a brisk run. Luckily, the countryside was close by and our exertions were fairly brief. We were presented with a different kind of landscape – wooded valleys met us instead of the flat countryside we had been passing through up until then. We came to a halt halfway up a slope next to a hedge which must have been very thick. The sky then soon presented us with its twice-daily performance. But our horizon was limited and the goal this time wasn't Eisenach. However, the air raid lasted for over two hours. Allied planes could now act brazenly like tourists. The material effect was slight but the effect on our spirits was huge…

We got back to the station like hikers. This air raid had upset the previous railway timetable. The track that we were supposed to take was reserved for more urgent transports. We were only able to leave towards the end of the afternoon. We weren't too crowded, fifty or sixty per wagon along with two or three Krauts. The sliding door also stayed slightly open. Our journey lasted three days, with little drama. It was even quite varied. The many air-raid warnings gave us the opportunity to visit the German countryside – generally very dull – and allowed us to relieve ourselves in decent fashion because we were more or less on our own, with a wooded copse standing in as a screen. Now we only lacked for one thing to complete our amazed contentment – and that was food. Rest made up for it.

TWELVE
BUCHENWALD

FROM ROLAND'S MEMOIR

On the evening of the third day, the night pitch black, we arrived at Buchenwald station. We were received in darkness and I couldn't make out our new horizon until we reached the main entrance. The road seemed flat as well as winding. The entrance drew us up short. We were lit up by a searchlight, made sinister by the thick fog that hung over this unimaginable place.

We waited for quite a long time. The cold was beginning to get its claws into us when finally, the gate opened. Yes, I say finally. Animals don't know how to deal with bad weather. They always seek shelter. They don't know how to discern if this shelter is a safe harbour or a hell. They enter in a confused way, sensing immediate safety. And so we crossed this threshold, we infiltrated this pound for men, this barn of starved sheep. The ground was irregular and sloped slightly, making it difficult to walk in the night.

From a tall chimney on our right, creepy flickers of light emerged at close intervals; the flames of hell were sucking on human pasture. A vague understanding dawned in us; the moment we had moved on past this hellish place, we had forgotten it.

The slope became steeper. We vaguely distinguished a row of buildings on our left, low, long, identical. There was no such symmetry on our right.

An abrupt right-angled turn led us to our first resting place. The light was put on; we entered an extended room which – I found out the following day – was the room where prisoners undressed. It was connected to a second, narrower room – 'the hairdressing salon'. These two rooms – bare, cold cement floors, no mattresses nor any straw – were soon covered with stretched-out bodies. The last men to enter struggled in vain to find a free spot. I was among them and quickly realised, faced with the evidence, that I wouldn't be able to stretch out. What to do? I found a stool; I saw an individual wash basin. My instinct, rather than thought, showed me a possible connection. I could put this seat in front of the basin, over a few feet and legs. I sat down and could doze with my head on my forearms resting on the basin. I was only partly undressed. I was woken up by the stifling tainted atmosphere of the place. I stripped down to my bare chest and went back to sleep. The night passed. When the wake-up call came, we were panting. The doors opened. We got dressed and were led into a livestock pen. This is the only term I can think of to describe this place accurately.

From this pen, a closed-in narrow corridor gave onto a disinfection building – the two rooms described above – then, to the side, the showers and the dressing room. A pallid misty morning quickly made us miss the overheated unhealthy atmosphere we had slept in. We came to a small part of the camp – less evocative in fact and the most presentable too: the kitchens, the clothes shop and beyond them, the blocks that we had glimpsed the evening before.

Between them and us, a space surrounded by barbed wire which seemed to be a place where blankets and laundry were spread out. In line with the strategy so dear to the hearts of this wretched people, we stayed exposed to the wind for several hours before disinfection began. This was the right of entry to the camp, so to speak. It was unavoidable and new arrivals always had to submit to it. It was a hygiene precaution – a tool for perfect hygiene I'd even say – but made pointless, ineffectual, absurd by what followed.

Counted in groups of ten, I think, at the exit from the passage to which we had all rushed, we passed into the first room. There we had to undress and make a small parcel of our rags with our registration number. Some foreign deportees piled them onto a wagon. Then we went into a 'hairdressing salon'. Multiple electric hair clippers hung from the ceiling.

Most of the workers were French. They accomplished their task like robots. The patient did not benefit from an ordinary armchair. He was seated for the haircut, but for the armpits and the chest, he had to stand up, and finally for the lower body, including the genitals, he had to climb onto a stool. Once we left that place, only filth remained.

A door opened once there were enough of us and we were in the showers. A *Crésyl*[42] disinfectant bath had been prepared for us. One by one, little by little, we had to immerse ourselves completely. Once we emerged, we were disinfected; even the dirt was clean. The hair clippers had left traces behind them, particularly where it had proved difficult. The disinfectant caused a sharp burning sensation on these scratches. Finally, we got into the showers – the water warm enough to clean us and cheer us up; we could take our time scrubbing one another without rushing. We had enough time, even though it was limited.

From there a second door opposite the first gave us access to a bright, spacious room where towels were handed out to us. These towels were often just bits of dish cloth, but nevertheless we were able to use them before giving them back. Then a painter, probably a house painter, armed with a big paintbrush, once again coated our shaved parts, paying special attention to those sought out by certain parasites. Then, still naked, we reached the clothing store, after having crossed through several rooms and a frozen corridor. The deportees still employed there gave each of us a pair of trousers, a shirt, a jacket. I forgot to say that we always kept our shoes – the only objects for which disinfection had been deemed pointless.

We met up again with some of our comrades, while others came to reinforce our group. Then we were led to the small camp, accompanied by a guide. A road made of large irregular cobblestones took us there. At this time, mud reigned everywhere; even the cobblestones were covered with it. A crudely constructed gate was opened and we entered the small camp. Nothing yet had been planned for our lodging. We had to wait. The spot chosen for us to wait was a third enclosure, the small camp's dumping ground so to speak. It was on a slope and, of course, received all the material and human waste from the camp.

....
42 Trademark of a disinfectant product.

Once we stopped, we surveyed the scene. The dilapidation of the surroundings, the filth of the place, the makeshift facilities, vast tents, ravaged individuals, none of this surprised us at all. Suffering was a fact of life for us and around us was only black suffering.

But against a partly collapsed wall there was a pile of naked, skeletal, withered corpses.

•

They looked as if they were part of the fallen debris. Piled up randomly one on top of the other, sometimes head to toe, their arms and legs often criss-crossed, they seemed to have been thrown there to serve as a sign in flesh to this quagmire. Our gaze rested there and yet not a single shudder signalled the fleeting awakening of our conscience. Not a single misgiving arose from our instinct for self-preservation. Nothing. We had been successfully reduced to a mindless state. This spectacle was proof of it.

The dog scents its brother's death but does not howl. It does not understand that this end is irreversible. Other movements attracted our attention. A handcart pulled by two deportees came to a stop next to a wooden cellblock.

The two men went inside and came out a few minutes later dragging a corpse. Then they took it, one by the feet, the other by the arms, and after a single swing back and forth – it weighed very little – threw it onto the platform. There was a dull, muffled thud. The skull and the wood collided. A second corpse joined the first. The load was now heavy enough because the path climbed upwards. What were these two prisoners? Undertakers no doubt. But how had they been able to end up with this scorn, this contempt for the dead? Habit perhaps? Stupidity? No. These two weren't weakened, they had double or triple rations. They weren't starving every hour of the day. They hadn't been reduced to a mindless state. I do not explain their behaviour. I acknowledge it, however. They made the most of their role without seeking to identify the horror of it.

Every morning several corpses were taken out of these designated quarantine blocks and placed – what am I saying? – they were thrown out at the entrance to the block. They were taken to the crematorium ovens a few days later when the relevant work squad was coming through this place.

Here and there in the middle of all the detritus, corpses in the mud, a few skeletal individuals used their last breath to get a little wood fire going under a box. This metal box no doubt contained a few scraps of potato or carrot retrieved carefully from the kitchen rubbish.

Our last comrades didn't take long to join us. A few hours later we were taken to our new lodging, a cellblock that looked the same as usual on the outside but was arranged on the inside to accommodate the maximum number of men. On each side, there was a series of 'boxes', between them an aisle about 2.3 to 3 metres wide. On one side the row of 'boxes' was interrupted. A space served as the inspection room. On the other side, the symmetry was disturbed by the cellblock chief's room, which lent a small note of decency in this pitiful dwelling.

Each box had three levels, one on top of the other. Each level was divided into two parts, left and right. Each part held twelve to sixteen men, one of whom acted as representative. Each of these sections was completely separate from the other. Each individual existed exclusively in his area.

The boxes were almost completely packed when we arrived. We didn't care much about our lodgings in any case. We had what counted most: a roof. Another idea preoccupied us: soup. We had not eaten in forty-eight hours. It was announced that we would have soup at the beginning of the afternoon. That was all we thought about. Finally, it arrived.

•

We were set to one side and the soup was distributed. This time it was dished out simultaneously from both ends of the temporary long mess hall. *Stubendienst* guards gave out mess kits to the first comers but there weren't enough. Once they had sucked up the soup, they passed on the mess kits to their comrades from the neighbouring boxes. Thus, the same set of utensils was used by four or five deportees without being washed. There was not even the most elementary level of cleanliness. We made light of the notion of one mess kit being used by someone ill, someone with tuberculosis, someone with dysentery, someone dying. The key thing was to get hold of it, fill it up and empty it as thoroughly as possible. Then we passed it on to the next person. Having eaten, I don't remember my afternoon timetable. I probably didn't sleep because I couldn't find any space and I hadn't yet managed to stretch myself out just anywhere, during the day at least.

In the evening our main concern was to find a vacant place to sleep in a sympathetic or at least neutral place. Our hunt was futile. I have to say though that our efforts were not that strenuous. The sleeping arrangements did not lend themselves to dreaming. The overcrowding of unfamiliar, pale, sickly people would have been enough to make a sane man nauseous. Somewhat used to it, we looked on indifferently at these recumbent bodies, these drained faces, these feverish impassioned discussions. But we hesitated to get in amongst these strange unsympathetic beings. They weren't our kind. We feared being scratched, bitten.

Finally, we found a table for our bed. My comrade and I, fused together, covered with our two blankets, managed to pass a reasonable night. We had also avoided the rest of the herd.

The next day, the twice-daily roll call took place. In this small camp, the roll calls took place outside the cell block and were done block by block. Discipline was less rigid. Each prisoner came out slowly, carrying his blanket which he put over his shoulders. Here it was tolerated.

Getting this scabies-ridden herd organised was difficult. We had to go backwards, forwards, fill in a gap, make more space. Finally, after twenty or thirty minutes of chaos, the herd was presentable. Then we waited for the German on duty to come. Once this was over, we were rid of this harsh chore. Immediately we rushed back to the block to get inside where the air was undoubtedly unhealthy and certainly foul-smelling, but warm. After some bland chit-chat, we went to stretch out on our table. During the morning, we had our first meal: bread and margarine. At first, we benefitted from pork fat by way of margarine, which was of American origin we were told, a feast to us. The spoonful granted to us was enough to give some taste to our revolting brown bread.

During the day we were free within a space of 400 square metres. We went outside as little as possible and always unwillingly. But we had to evacuate the block to allow it to be sluiced down. In any case it only took half an hour to carry out this useless task. Then we hastily returned to our wet hovel.

Such opportunities caused unaccustomed activity in the toilets. We all ended up there. This place was indeed the best flea market. Cigarettes were the standard currency there, as they were everywhere. You could get clothes, carrots, spoons, bread – in fact, everything our very limited imagination and our even more meagre wishes could desire.

This communal toilet was definitely unique. It was located in a building identical to all the others but only occupied half of it. The other part was reserved for the washrooms, also communal. I never used them, however. I cleaned myself, very cursorily I must say, using a simple outside tap fixed on the side wall of our block. This toilet was a ditch with slanting walls forming an angle of about 50 degrees. Several planks ran along this ditch, one of which provided a back. This avoided the risk of falling. A fairly narrow passageway meant you could look for a sheltered spot. The walls constituted the urinal.

After a few days of this unimaginable existence, we had adapted to this new environment.

We also learnt the tricks of how this vast camp was run. We learnt specifically that this huge camp received Red Cross parcels that we had always been deprived of. We decided to go and visit the Frenchman responsible for the distribution of these parcels. A comrade and I were delegated to go on this occasion. We took advantage of a summons from our Eisenach *Kommando* to the labour office to seek out on our return the block where the fortunate bestower of these precious goods lived. We found him and outlined our grievances to him. We realised that each man's portion was inadequate, miniscule, but we knew that being allocated the least little treat without any great material value would have a great effect on the morale of these diminished, apathetic beings. In this way they would understand that their pitiful fate was known and that some fellow countrymen, even though miserable themselves, were trying to mitigate their complete destitution.

We advanced these arguments. Unfortunately, death's anteroom was not a meaningless image. First of all, the Krauts objected to these handouts. What didn't they object to? But most of all we were looked upon as dying men whose coming fate was not in doubt. Why therefore waste food which would be far more useful for others who were fitter? Why allow a smile, a last smile of contentment on a face that by tomorrow would no longer even bear this feverish expression of earthly damnation? Why have any pity, why? And yet several vague promises were made to us.

We went back sheepishly and reported on our interview. For a few days, we were sustained by a vague hope, then this prospect of a piece of sugar, of a few dry cakes disappeared.

Our monotonous stay was interrupted by various communal meetings. None of them was favourably received. We preferred the unhealthy warmth of a foul barn to long waits exposed to the wind in which, scarcely dressed, we froze without shivering. We assumed that future assignments would come to put an end to our lazy life and take us out of our present sordid state. Even so, despite the relative inactivity of the small camp, we all wished to leave it as quickly as possible. First of all the nagging hunger, then the daily spectacle of death, lowered the spirits of even the toughest. Every morning a few corpses were removed from the boxes. They were transported on a stretcher and deposited outside where the special detail carted them to the crematorium. One of them even stayed a whole day on his stretcher, left at the base of a box near the entrance doorway. He only stood out from the rest of us by his stillness and his silence.

By about the tenth day since our arrival at Buchenwald, each box was required to draw up the list of its inmates in the form of registration numbers, through the intermediary of its representative. We were told it was for the forthcoming distribution of coats. What a godsend, we thought, even though we only expected to get the usual striped jacket in shameful colours. Meanwhile, we had been obliged to abandon our basic sleeping area for another box which was partly stripped. Luckily, we had formed a French team and so we were able to settle in without too many clashes. Our nights however were disturbed. We were stuck to each other and so couldn't move, or as little as possible. Every time someone got up during the night he woke us up. In these moments of mental clarity, the atmosphere of the room revealed itself in many forms.

Installed at the entry to the box, in the pale light of the night lights I discerned bodies stretched out on benches – a few were even on the floor. Other deportees wearing their blankets walked slowly in the temporarily empty or even deserted aisle. No snoring, the occasional shouting out, often moans, and sometimes calls for help. Persistent, ruthless battles took place at the dark end of one tier. What was the reason for these battles? A bit of bread had awoken envy in a starving man? The owner defended his pittance with an unimaginable rage. Even a kick delivered by a disturbed sleeper prompted a brutal reaction which degenerated into a brawl.

Even during the day when soup was being distributed, there were clashes. Once I saw a tall, emaciated, bony lad punching his neighbour fiercely, a sickly, prematurely aged being whose only defence was to protect his face with his folded arms. What was the reason for this punishment – an attempted theft or a bid to benefit from a second ration?

•

One evening the distribution of the greatcoats took place. The numbers had been sewn onto the overcoats in the *Effektenkammer* [clothing stock room] and had been allocated without any preliminary fitting. Not that this mattered much. They began to call out the numbers; the overseer was luck, good or bad.

Some unlucky ones only got the basic striped jacket, luckier ones got three-quarter length coats, very warm but not long enough; finally, the luckiest were those blessed by chance who got a real coat.

I was one of these. Fate had smiled on me. I received a foreign-made raglan, Czech I think; the material was thick and the coat almost new, or nearly. Without doubt it had belonged to a Jew whose life had been prematurely and brutally cut short. I put it on for the night and the feel of the wooden board was less harsh. The next day, I faced the morning roll call fearlessly. Hands in pockets, collar turned up, it seemed to me that I no longer inspired pity. Then we were sent in small groups to the transfer blocks.

Our move to the transfer block gave rise to a scene that was at the same time odd, moving and excessively grand. The void that our departure was going to create was to be filled with a group of young Jews recently arrived from a place perhaps even more terrible than Buchenwald. They were waiting outside. We were called out individually by our registration numbers and formed a second crowd.

Night had fallen. A stormy cloud-filled sky made it profoundly dark. The electric lighting set above the door only penetrated a limited area, despite its shocking brightness. Our group grew bigger. Suddenly the lamps went out, plain darkness reigned. Then even more bleakly in this black night, the siren wailed its harsh lament. The transfer block's door was closed again to avoid an invasion that would have cancelled out the work done up to that point. There were about 100 of us outside, including sixty Jews. An icy, stormy wind blew. The thunderstorm was fast approaching. Low rumblings, then fat raindrops sowed panic among us. Each of us huddled with his neighbour, seeking shelter. In the distance, the sky was criss-crossed with flashes of lightning. The splendid indomitable storm was rushing in. Swept by the wind, the rain hit our sides full on. The storm had arrived.

A groan arose from the shifting, shapeless group. The young Jews, frozen and terrified, let out a rhythmic piteous moan. Soon we could make out a second roaring; it grew louder, flew over our heads. The squadron was beginning its invisible nocturnal demonstration. Two thunderstorms joined forces to destroy and terrify us. The ground was booming now, sending up dazzling sprays. Light took it in turns to come down from the sky and rise up from the earth.

To a certain kind of mind, the show might have appeared spectacular, sometimes heavenly, sometimes hellish…

Without being aware of it, for a few seconds I enjoyed such a display, but the icy rain continued to pierce us with thousands of darts. The moaning became more strident, more prolonged.

The least exposed walls of the building sheltered a part of our bodies but not much. The space that ran the length between the two buildings was swept by whirlwinds of rain. Sometimes man and nature seemed to be battling it out. The lightning and the artillery flashes were competing for which could be brightest. Thunder cracks and the rat-tat-tat of machine guns sought mutually to outdo each other. Yet nature seemed more jittery, more feline, its flashes were sharp and unexpected like scratches. The roaring lasted for less time, sounded hoarse. A strange calm followed its response; even the wind and the rain fell silent. This spectacle in all its grandeur weighed heavily on our frail shoulders. Far from comforting us, this power which diminished man seemed to subdue us even more. The rain and the wind continued their concert and although we didn't hear it, we felt its effects.

Suddenly, I realised that our group had become a lot smaller. I looked around my surroundings as best I could and I noticed some shadows loping off.

I understood that the toilet block was the main attraction of the moment. This was often the case anyway. I rushed over there and experienced huge relief once inside. In fact I was astonished that it had taken us over half an hour to think of this heaven-sent shelter.

The two hurricanes seemed to have calmed down. You could hear the wind's menacing howling. The fierce rain shattered angrily against the wall or came in vehemently through the door-less entrance way under our roof. After around two hours or so of waiting, the end of the air-raid siren sounded. The storm had subsided too. We went back to our block; the wide-open door allowed a fuzzy light to emerge along with some precious heat. To our astonishment we were able to go back in. The late hour meant no more legal activities were allowed. We lay down for a final night on our sides. The young Jews settled down too, I don't know where nor how. Exhausted by these strong emotions, I fell deeply asleep.

One evening I finally left this accursed little camp and along with about twenty of my comrades, I was led to a new dwelling. It was a one-storey building constructed out of stones. There I found an individual bed and a straw mattress. Decent flushing toilets with individual seats. The space was quite confined but nevertheless good enough. But there were countless fleas and lice in this place. The day following our arrival, a section of our group was assigned to go on clearance duty in Weimar. An entire train carried a thousand men every day to this town 9km outside the camp. They were divided into multiple teams, each one responsible for disposing of debris, recovering furniture, food supplies etc.

Some had the unexpected luck of being responsible for clearing out a bakery or a cake shop. In the evening, the lucky ones from this squad returned cheerful and full of hope for the following days. Many volunteered when they heard about these fantastic discoveries. I was extremely reluctant when I was assigned automatically. And the next day I and my companions were woken up at four in the morning to go to the roll call before departure.

The night was black. The vast assembly square was swept by an icy north wind. Spotlights cast wide beams of light. Little by little various groups formed, a headcount was carried out and once the right number of men had been selected, those left over went back to their 'home'.

We arrived quickly at the nearby station. Numerous guards made up our escort. A train was waiting for us. Those who were used to it quickly filled up the wagons. The new ones stayed on the platform. There were about fifty of us and none of the teams who had already been assembled for some time wanted us. Finally, we were fitted in here and there. The darkness was still just as black.

The train departed. Crammed into the wagons, we could doze standing up. After several stops, we reached our destination. Dawn had replaced the night. We got out of the wagons in a rush. Each man hastily joined up with his section. The good *Kommandos* were full and didn't need any reinforcements. The group I was assigned to did not have a specific duty. It drifted here and there according to need. That day we followed the rail track and reached the sorting yards. We were made to stop by a briquette depot – peat briquettes I think. We had to lift these briquettes into some wagons. We were armed with forks that had many long, curved prongs. The work wasn't interesting because we couldn't unearth anything to eat.

A few air raids came to liven up our sad situation. We joyfully abandoned this thankless chore to end up in the neighbouring countryside. Our searching gaze didn't discover anything that could appease our ravenous hunger. We were in a forest whose sparse flora gave us barely any protection. And yet here it seemed less windy, the air milder. Unfortunately, the end of the air raid forced us to leave this rural retreat to go back to our task.

The day was long. The fresh air aroused our hunger. However, we had to wait for the return to camp to get our daily ration. We enthusiastically welcomed the end of work. The return to the camp was the same as coming to work. On this occasion once again, we wished for a rapid return to our hovel so we could have our meagre pittance. I had also been put to the Weimar test.[43] I wasn't proud about it and wished to be able to avoid it the next day. I slept heavily. The physical effort, the fresh air, the early morning rising had all exhausted me. However, like the day before, I had to get up very early and after getting my breakfast – 300gm of bread and some margarine that I devoured immediately – I had to go to roll call.

I tried hard with a few comrades to stay in the last rows of my column to take advantage of there being too many workers if this situation arose.

....
43 *Faire l'épreuve de Weimar* – possibly this refers to the heavy bombing by Allied forces.

Unfortunately, our ruse was pointless and I had to embark for the second time but this time against my wishes. We arrived at Weimar at dawn just like the previous day where I had to join the coal *Kommando* again. And I couldn't avoid it. A few tried to get into better squads but always in vain. They were on the receiving end of blows from both the *Kapo* and our guards and ultimately had to go back to the first tasks they were assigned to.

This second day, however, brought me some consolation. The morning air raid had sent us into the countryside. In the middle of vast fields some distance away, a huge barn spread out its black bulk across a gloomy landscape. The path we were following brought us closer to it. A track allowed us to go alongside it. An opening gave us access to it. Our column extended over more than 200 metres. Our herd had been thoroughly tamed and running away was no longer a risk.

The first ones there, me among them, were therefore able to poke around in the barn at their leisure. We discovered a pile of partially frozen or rotten fodder beets. We set aside the spoilt tubers on top with our hands to get at the better ones beneath. I took four or five beets this way that I stashed inside my jacket as best I could. Anyway, the guards who had arrived by now and been warned of our discovery didn't react and let the latecomers load up. I thought I would be able to appease my hunger without fear. But no, alas fodder beets are barely edible. The bitter taste was really not at all appetising. Even so I ate a few bits then put them away so I could try to cook them at the worksite. I knew where to find the necessary fire there.

Upon our return, I headed over to a 'drainage' pit where a driver was just then cleaning out the congested furnace of his locomotive. A pile of hot ashes and burning coals were just the job for what I wanted to do. I sat astride the rail track, against a drive wheel and leaned my body towards this source of heat. I tucked my beets underneath the ashes and returned to my work. A quarter of an hour later I went back to look at my dish. I crouched down in the same spot and began to retrieve a beet when a whistle sounded. I didn't take any notice, but suddenly the locomotive moved forwards. Luckily, it set off slowly. An automatic reflex saved me. I was leaning towards the ditch so let myself fall in and thus avoided my leg being cut in two which would have been as fatal as the guillotine blade. A few seconds afterwards, I stood up without even a burn on me as the train continued its journey.

A Kraut who had witnessed this scene from afar and who had rushed forward to help me back on my feet – perhaps – was very surprised to see me get up by myself. He hurled abuse at me I think, but I didn't even try to understand him.

I went back to the pit, took my half-cooked beets and went back quietly to my post. Had I understood the danger that had just brushed me by? I don't think so. And there's no doubt I would have gone back again to cook them properly with the same dedication, if one of our guards who had been tipped off hadn't come – not to forbid me with many threats not to expose myself to great danger, but not to leave work.

With my beets now cooked, I could assuage my hunger. This pathetic discovery was enough to encourage me and to make this journey to Weimar almost worthwhile. Over the next few days I didn't try any tricks to avoid it. I could bring back a dozen of these choice foods in an old bag I found on the rail track. In the wagon I exchanged two beets against a spoon and in the block, I swapped several others for a mismatched pair of fingerless mittens. One was of different-coloured bits of wool but well made, the other had been crudely fashioned from a bit of khaki-coloured army material. It turned out that this unforeseen exchange was of great help to me. Finally, that evening I had another cigarette. I promised myself to bring back lots of beets the next day and with this in mind I hid my bag carefully under the straw mattress at the head end.

Unfortunately, the next day after feeling very hopeful because I was in the same *Kommando*, I was completely crestfallen when I realised at the first air-raid warning that we were changing direction for the second time. We went to a wooded area where, despite looking carefully, I didn't find anything, not even a poisonous mushroom. This time I was fed up with Weimar. Furthermore, our stay at the transit block was to be very brief. It simply preceded our deployment to the big camp. And one evening, after a miserable and fruitless day, I learnt that I was allocated to block number 32 I think (in the big camp), with four of my companions. We went there immediately and were surprised to find out that our arrival had not yet been announced. The *Stubendienst* boss [barrack-room duty boss] allocated us a bunk and seeing us empty-handed asked us if we had had our daily ration. When we replied in the affirmative, he was astonished to realise that already I had nothing left. Sustained by his job, he seemed to have forgotten that hunger is a dominant instinct. Lucky those who didn't let themselves get dragged into degrading acts. How many in these camps lost all their dignity.

Everyone there endured the ordeal of deprivation, of mental distress. Rich or poor, this time for the most part at least, equality reigned. And this latest ordeal taught each one of us what deprivation is, and what the moral consequences are. May they never forget it and strive each day to banish this scourge from our earth. The memories of their own misery must be brought back to life when they see the destitution of others.

The hungry beggar must pierce the heart of one who has known long-term starvation. Deprivation can only be understood by the deprived. The camps made it familiar to many. So much so that they awoke in us a feeling that was perhaps too violent, but legitimate when justified: hatred.

I curse those who feel sorry for the fate of the Germans and only wish a fair punishment for them. They should experience the camps. Then their compassion will transform into unbridled hate. My hatred has a limit, nevertheless; it stops when confronted with early childhood. But the adult has no gender, no age, no soul.

And so I was placed in the big camp. The atmosphere seemed healthier. The block's layout was designed better. Our entourage didn't appear to be starving, at least in general. We took our meals on a table, we even had use of large china bowls. They were shared but a nearby sink meant we could wash them. This big camp's only disadvantage was the daily roll call. It took place in the large square between 18:30 and 19:00 hours and, including preliminaries, lasted at least an hour. In the morning we returned to our respective *Kommandos* after the regular alarm.

Our *Arbeiter*, another name for supervisor and synonymous with *Kapo*, counted his workforce, noted the absentees and waited for the moment of departure. It took place at six o'clock on the dot and was accompanied by an unexpected ritual which surprised me greatly. A *Kommando* of musicians formed a noisy marching band with a limited repertoire. They took up their positions near the main door on the right along the side of the road, and on the signal for departure they began to play heaven knows what piece. For about 200 metres we had to obey the tempo, even sometimes the rhythm of the music. In the evening at 18:00 hours, the same thing happened on our return from work. Once we passed through the gateway, we scattered to our respective blocks with a certain amount of haste. In fact, we wanted to eat our daily soup ration before the evening roll call.

Again, on this occasion I had some luck. I was assigned to the *Kommando Bahnhof* [train station squad] the advantages of which I was able to appreciate later. Initially considered as strong labourers, oh irony, we benefitted from three weekly additional snacks. This was an unexpected godsend. This supplement in effect virtually doubled our daily ration. Our work didn't require any more effort than that of most of the other squads, but perhaps there was some practical side to it that many of the others didn't have.

We had to sink cement posts to install an electric line. This construction site began at the Weimar-Buchenwald line terminus, which was a railway line dead end. We witnessed here the army of convoys, a sad spectacle that we had experienced ourselves and which left us unmoved.

But we also watched the arrival of supply trains – potatoes, cabbages, swedes, carrots and fodder carrots. Then the boldest abandoned their work and eagerly sought out supplies, despite the threat from the *Lagerschutz* [the camp police], deportees themselves. I remember teaming up with a young Russian with a slight limp who was a past master in this business. He took advantage too of the *Arbeiter*'s benevolent inattentiveness. He could therefore leave his work with impunity, signalling to me when a train arrived, and disappearing. He would soon come back and unload the fruits of his petty theft into my care. He set off again immediately on the look-out for the opportune moment to leap onto a wagon and relieve it again of a tiny portion of its contents. When there was absolutely no more opportunity to evade surveillance, he came back, took his booty after having given me a share of course, and went off to make his lavish meal, which the *Arbeiter* also benefitted from.

When I also got hold of a couple of potatoes, I tried hard – often in vain – to cook them on the coals. The fire that I had built so painstakingly would become the focus of concerted monitoring. The excess of smoke could lead to discovery by the surveillance Kraut; the approach of any guard meant I had to put it out quickly. But my half-cooked potatoes were a very enviable treat. On one occasion indeed, I managed to steal two white cabbages myself. I feasted on them right away and never – up to that moment or since – have I appreciated this edible vegetable so much. The leaves were white and tender, the juicy stalks crunched as I chewed them. This was Buchenwald's *belle époque*. Work there was not constantly supervised.

The hole we had to dig to put in the posts was a fine shelter, both from the wind and from the prying eyes of our masters. We could observe without being seen, backs against the damp clay walls, sitting on a large rock or standing when the hole was deep. The moment the enemy approached, the spade was once again in motion and throwing out a few stones or a few recalcitrant clods of earth.

But unfortunately, I had to leave this interesting work for a more urgent task. Flat railcars loaded with earth had been brought along an isolated track. Their contents were to be used to backfill the side of a mound. Perched on these wagons, we had to unload them. Exposed to the winds we commanded the camp's broad avenue. Several times a day we witnessed a passing tractor pulling a trailer. It was a mortuary/death convoy. The crematorium, working at a reduced rate because of the lack of coal and especially because of the numbers of dead, was no longer able to cope with the incineration of the corpses.

•

How many corpses did I see? Poor wasted, naked, dead bodies. Your nakedness could not appear indecent even to the inexperienced eye. Your hollow cheeks, your concave breasts, your limbs where the skin barely covered the bones, offered very little for the ovens to feast on.

In the last days, the lack of coal put an end to the burning of the bodies. Their burial place was even more wretched. Corpses by the hundred were chucked into communal pits and doused with quicklime.

How many perished from a bullet in the back of the neck, their bodies dumped by the side of the track, during the final transports? At least a bullet to the back of the neck might have been quicker than a blow from the butt of a gun to a dying person's skull.

•

The proximity of uncultivated land supplied us with a new resource. Many dandelions had grown on this abandoned land, partly field, partly marshland. As soon as the moment was favourable, always the boldest went to collect this plentiful harvest, chests thrust forward – and I was one of them this time. Never throughout my life in liberty have I found such beautiful dandelions! A few breaks were enough for us to get a medium harvest. Then we prepared them, took off the yellowing leaves and earth. When we got back to camp, we cleaned them in running water and, after having cut them up into pieces, added them to the soup as soon as it was served. The thin soup grew thick and took on a bit of bulk.

The air raids, as ever, were welcome. They brought about a completely unforeseen and legal chaos. The moment the warning sounded all the deportees working outdoors ran back at the double to the camp. The door was wide open and a few guards on duty at the entrance made everyone speed up without doing a headcount. This spectacle was even more astonishing, at least for the first few times, given the way entrances and exits were carried out so methodically with strict headcounts of the workers. Once the air raid was over, the various *Kommandos* reformed and our departure took place in the same way as in the morning, but without music this time.

Buchenwald was already razed to the ground so could no longer be the target of the bombing. But Weimar had only been partially affected and remained a target to hit. The Allied squadrons frequently did nothing but fly over the region, albeit in large numbers, which meant long periods of rest for us.

Our stay in the large camp did not bring us the mental comfort that we expected, even though it brought us an undeniable improvement in our physical conditions. From the very first days we realised that our pathetic state did not excite any particular sympathy, nor any pity.

For communal meals the workforce in the block was divided among eight tables, fifteen to eighteen units (men) per table. Leftovers were distributed per table in rotation, like the Red Cross parcels. A blackboard showed the number of the table that was going to benefit from these leftovers. However, there was no confusion about the narrow range of dishes that normally constituted our menu. It made sense that you couldn't randomly share out leftovers of rutabaga [swede] soup, potato soup or boiled potatoes. So each of these foods had to be dished out in a specific order which was marked up on the blackboard, like a racing board. We were unpleasantly surprised to find that our turn had just passed for each one of these dishes.

Was this by chance? Perhaps, I'll admit. However, in this case someone could have done us a justifiable favour and given us a first go at the leftovers.

Our resentment was further fuelled by a later distribution of Red Cross parcels. We definitely understood the reality then. The table benefitting from these treats was precisely the one that preceded us. We were left in no doubt; chance could not be more selfish than man. The table which was made up mostly of our group witnessed both the arrival and the departure of this distribution at the same time. Through sheer chance, this table was considered as a point of departure and excluded from this undeniable benefit of boundless sharing.

With what envious eyes we watched the contents of these parcels being laid out. What shudders must have run down the spine of many when they saw this pile of French cigarette packs – which we hadn't tasted for a year – within reach on the neighbouring table. And these treats which dazzled us: gingerbread, fruit jellies, dehydrated vegetables and dried beans – not a bit of which we would get. We weren't even offered a single cigarette as consolation. Ah, brotherhood, what a load of nonsense here – or in this world, I should say. These parcels were rare, for from now on deliveries were unusual. We would have to wait almost a month before our turn came around.

And on that day, what joy! We had feared so much that we wouldn't taste them, these delectable delicacies. A parcel for ten. It wasn't much but enough for us. A few cubes of sugar, a slice of gingerbread, a chunk of chocolate, a tin of sardines for three or four and finally, dried vegetables which we didn't share out. We would make a delicious communal soup out of them.

We made our way slowly towards the end of our suffering. The crucial period was approaching. The number of air raids was increasing and work was interrupted several times each day. The Allies were coming closer. One last time, the air raid caught us at work. We swiftly returned. We would only get out again either as liberated men or heading towards our death.

•

This time two-thirds of the camp workers, some 40,000 unfortunates, went towards a tragic death. The final third had the unique luck of staying behind and being liberated there.

No longer being forced to work gave us much comfort. We were thus better able to conserve our waning strength. Daily life was the same except for our extra snacks and some dandelion supplements. Our physical state ought to have felt more bearable. Unfortunately, our mental state was severely tested during this period. The coming liberation for which we all wanted to stay alive had revitalised our failing hearts, had ignited a spark in our feeble spirits.

We finally understood quite clearly that from now on any retreat would give rise to an intentional punitive slaughter, i.e. a collective assassination, or for a natural slaughter, i.e. a legal one, an authorised execution of the weak. This last procedure which would not in any way have worsened the Germans' reputation, would have been enough to kill off four out of five of the convoys and of course, this was all we could imagine.

Convoys departed each day. Generally, they included 5,000 men. What an atmosphere of dread, of fear, of terror reigned then. What efforts we made, futile for the most part, to avoid, to delay a death to which we had been indifferent up until then. The imminence of salvation had given us back the taste for life. However, the numbers had to be kept up. Age, nationality, health – none of these mattered. The strongest, the most cunning in our world of the sickly found, however, a way of disappearing from the roll call location and getting back to a shelter where they would temporarily be forgotten. Once the danger had passed, they reappeared for the daily soup. The next day was an exact copy of the day before down to the smallest detail.

The days passed. The guns boomed constantly. The aeroplanes flew over our miserable camp continuously. Each day witnessed the birth and death of hope. Each day 5,000 men left for an uncertain destination, unknown perhaps, but one which would never be reached.

THIRTEEN

WILL WE MAKE IT?

FROM ROLAND'S MEMOIR

My block received the order to be ready. We were advised to take only what was strictly necessary so as not to be overloaded. Each of us was busy for a moment, and very quickly the light burden was ready. Meantime, by common and tacit consent we decided not to answer the order to assemble at the designated roll call location. We had no idea what the consequences might be, but we hoped thereby to gain some precious moments.

The order came, we stayed where we were, passive; this could be our only defence.

On that day, however, our departure was deferred.

The next day our block was forgotten. Others had to submit themselves to the now mandatory roll call. A group of fellow countrymen came to seek refuge under our roof which offered temporary protection.

We were just sitting at our respective tables and sadly contemplating the gravity of the moment. We were at the same moment on the threshold of life and the threshold of death. Any little thing was enough either to finish us off suddenly or to rekindle the flickering flame, the last breath of life which was left in us.

We could do nothing faced with this incredible enigma. A renewed passivity could not and would not be useful. We understood this in a confused way. If it turned out there was no escape, we would have to obey and go to face our destiny. So, our companions went back to our dormitory and we continued to hope we would get out of this bloody tragedy unscathed.

The day passed. The guns were always booming and always seemed to be at the gateway of our sorrows. The aeroplanes furrowed the sky in all directions. Their wings sparkled in the prematurely spring-like sky. All of nature declared renewal to us and yet how many had already perished. The azure blue sky bathed us in its luminous brightness. The warm rays were intent on giving us the life that men wanted to take from us. But alas, evil always vanquishes good. Kindness is merely a feeble stem which bends endlessly in the perverse winds of wickedness.

•

The end of the day took a long time to arrive.

Our comrades had gone back to their block. It had already been several days since the siren had sounded. The air raid was continuous. Each evening the same question remained: what will tomorrow bring? Each hour which passed brought us closer to the conclusion. In the evening at least, this conclusion was a positive one: we had made it through another day. In the morning, however, we could only see the downside. Despite everything, our nights were calm. Our soothing slumbers were never troubled by any nightmare.

Just like past dawns, the dawn of April 10th found us ready to undergo the supreme test – and I was still hopeful that we would avoid it. The morning passed without incident. At the beginning of the afternoon the much-feared order to assemble sounded ominously in our ears. This time we had to obey. Each man got ready slowly and a first group formed in front of our block. We knew that nothing good could come of this last departure, we guessed that we either had to accept our fate passively or rebel and attempt the impossible. This was what we focused on.

We decided to walk a few kilometres to put distance between ourselves and the camp, then to try to take down our armed escort. The task was not going to be easy because we were so weak. And yet a final burst from each one of us could allow us to hope for a favourable outcome. We were ten against one and if we acted together, with the advantage of surprise, it seemed to us that our plan would not necessarily end up in deadly failure. Each line had their chief. We were thus shipshape in front of the block and waiting for the ultimate roll call. It was a long time coming. We sat down on what served as pavements which delimited the road. One hour went by.

The hope of some eleventh-hour obstacle or other took hold. It was confirmed by the silence from the command post where the orders came from. We went back to our mattresses. The daylight slowly faded and the evening once again found us in the camp.

•

This dramatic day, the most tragic of our year-long exile, had ended. We felt that the next day could only be the long-awaited day of liberty regained, or on the contrary, the wretched – and most likely bloody – end to a long dying. We had been too tested over such a long time to be filled, according to our natures, either with mad hope or with deep despair. We were unmoved as we waited for the last day to dawn. Our night was calm and restful, just like the previous nights. We were still sleeping when dawn arrived to wake us up. Just like every other morning, we appreciated getting up slowly and dawdling, although this was fleeting as our pests reminded us of our daily duties. Having drunk our coffee and had a wash, we subsided onto our respective benches to wait for the unforeseeable which, despite everything, we hoped would be positive.

I have forgotten what we were chatting about specifically, but for sure it was about the joyous, shiny, affluent future which was coming, and then of course the usual song and dance about the lavish yet delicate food. No more promises of shared visits. The bright sunlight had invaded our hovel. The day was going to be radiant. The most heavenly blue sky was a sublime backdrop against which these gods of the sky glided in such perfect formation. For now they were coming around the clock, without hindrance, to announce more certainly than any Messiah the imminent end of our suffering…

We had gone outside in spite of the ban, which we'd ignored for almost ten days, to admire the silvered reflections of the Allied aircraft. They seemed to be harmless tourists by now. On this spring day only the regular blasts of the cannon persisted, reminding us of the war. No orders issued forth from the entry post. For the first time the camp had lost the panting rhythm of these last days. It seemed to have been assailed by an overwhelming indolence. We too were quiet on that radiant day, giving no sign of the strength of our feelings. Our bodies seemed apathetic, shapeless, made languid by the heat of an early spring. We felt that nature was showing us such compassion that we couldn't be defeated.

Despite the many dashed hopes, we were waiting for the end of that day which felt a world away from our imprisonment. The afternoon that followed was as beautiful as the morning. I believe there had never been such pleasantly spring-like weather to adorn the harshness of Germany…

We started to feel a quiver of anxiety as we slumped on our benches, forearms on the table. We knew that darkness fell quickly despite the brightness of the hour, and the shadows signalled for us the end of another day which still would not bring us back our freedom. It was in this indefinable atmosphere that we were surprised by an unusual roaring from the siren. It announced: 'Enemy tanks in sight'. The long-awaited moment was here, the moment for which thousands of human beings had not had the strength to survive, was finally here. We were advised to stay calm. But was that necessary? Hadn't fourteen months of starvation been enough to take from us all our energy, our ability to react? Our muscles weren't destroyed, they were simply slack. The only strength we had left enabled us simply to breathe more deeply – better, it seemed.

And then, we saw planes, we heard tanks. They had to be right there on the spot to be able, finally, to deliver us…

•

End of Roland Chopard's memoir. The date was 11 April 1945.

Note: Roland was one of 21,160 deportees held in the camp on that fine spring day, which Christian Bernadac reconstructs in detail through the testimonies of various witnesses.[44]

----

44 Christian Bernadac (1995). *La Libération des Camps*. Paris: Éditions Michel Lafon.

FOURTEEN
COMING HOME

LETTER HOME FROM ROLAND

Dear everyone

Finally, we have been delivered from the German yoke and everyone tells us that it won't be long before we are sent home.

I hope that everyone is well, that Dad is back in France, and that my little Alex is sturdy and strapping. I don't want to keep asking questions as this letter doesn't need a reply, at least not a written one.

So I'll just talk about me. At the beginning, my life in Germany was just about bearable even though we worked under continual beatings from the Kapos and the SS. The Kapos were people like us, but who had been in the camps for several years, even up to ten years and more. Then I was posted to a factory where work was not hard but long – 12-hour days, working night and day, all week. I was in charge of checking parts, work that of course was botched. Months went by, the new year arrived, military events escalated, and Germany finally reached a critical stage. We endured the first repercussions. Our rations got progressively meagre, and we were wasting away. We were evacuated from Eisenach and sent to Buchenwald. I will describe life there when I see you again… Then with the Allied advance, the Americans were soon at our gates. We had several truly anxious days. There could have been another evacuation. Had it taken place, it would have cost the lives of hundreds, maybe thousands of men, because many among us were old and weak.

Finally, the nightmare of the last days came to an end on the afternoon of April 11th.

From the next day we got better food and now we are eating normally.

I am desperate to hug you all tight, to see France again, to get home at last to my family.

And Christian…? But there I go, asking you questions again, which is pointless. If a reply were to make its way to me, then let it be a real journal…

I'm going to stop writing now, finally, so that you can stop worrying about me. I am alive, well and indescribably happy at the thought of seeing you soon. I am sending you all thousands of kisses – to Moncany, grandparents, Aunt Léa…

Roland

•

IRÈNE REPLIES
Fumel
27th April 1945

My beloved

I can't find enough superlatives to describe to you my immense happiness, my overflowing joy, when I learnt of your liberation, nor can I describe to you my equally great joy when, the day before yesterday, I was able to read my dearest Roland's handwriting. Oh I am *so* happy, what immeasurable happiness I am feeling, and how impatient I am to see you again, to be with you again, to tell you over and over how much I love you and to be able to hug you so much that you will beg for 'mercy'.

My Uncle Emile was the one who came at midnight to tell us of your liberation. I will explain it all to you in person – then in the morning at the factory, three other people confirmed the news, then your letter came, this letter that is so dear to me and that I know by heart… and now I am waiting for you darling, come back quickly, really quickly and send me a telegram as soon as you arrive in Paris.

'If a reply were to make its way to me, then let it be a real journal…'

A real journal… you will find it once you are back home… I can't explain it to you… but first of all I am going to tell you that my brother is in Paris, at the École des Travaux Publics [Public Works College]. His address in town is: 90 Rue Emile Raspail in Arcueil. He has gone to give them the address at the reception centre at the Quai d'Orsay. Go see him if you can but don't spend too long with him. Think of us, send me a telegram to tell us you've arrived.

The whole family is well and happy, and thrilled that you are coming home as you can tell.

I didn't want to start with bad news, but I have to tell you that my dear father died on the 25th of July. Alex and I were with him… I will explain so many things to you. The poor man, he was counting so much on seeing you again before he died… now he will not know that happiness, for underneath his frosty exterior, he loved you so much.

Your little Alex is a beautiful, healthy, lively boy, but wild. He often calls to you, he knows you (from the photos) and I never put him to bed without giving him your picture, he kisses you then holds it out to me so that I can kiss you too, then he laughs, and I put him to bed. Our little *Titou* is naughty, but so cute, soon you will see for yourself. If I was sure this letter would reach you, I would send a photo.

Your father has still not returned, probably towards the end of June according to his last letter. We have got to know each other (on paper) and he writes me charming letters. Lucienne is thinking of setting off in May because Paul is ill and Jackie is tired. Your mother has been a little unwell at times but, as always – her dizzy spells.

I have been so unhappy, if only I could tell you how much I have suffered so far from you… I prefer not to talk to you about it because this terrible nightmare is coming to an end… but at least I had my

Titou and my family. I wasn't alone like some prisoners' wives. I've always worked, I'm still working, and I will take my leave when you are home. I am saving a surprise for you – maybe several…

I wish you a Happy Birthday my darling, you turned 28 on 21st April. I was thinking that perhaps you might be home. I put flowers everywhere, the house was like a mirror… But it was postponed… but don't dally too much my beloved, I am so eager to see you again. I love you so much, my Roland, my darling husband. I have prayed for you so much; every Sunday at 6.30 in the morning, my mother and I took communion thinking of you, and God has answered our prayers and I have thanked him with all my heart. You will see that there are certain happy coincidences…

All my office colleagues will be happy to see you again. I will stop now, my darling, in the hope that I will receive a telegram rather than a letter, or even better, that I will see *you*.

The whole family sends their love. *Titou* is blowing big kisses to his darling daddy and your 'little darling' hugs you warmly, passionately, and never stops saying 'I love you, I love you.' Come back to me soon darling. Come back quickly and we can start to live happily together again, the three of us.

Your Irène who loves you madly,

Irène

PS

I am no longer the whimsical little Irène that I was, this separation has made me grow up; if I have ever wronged you, I sincerely ask for your forgiveness. I have to say I'm sorry, I was just a child, but this ordeal has made my love stronger, and you will see, darling, that we are going to be so happy, we won't ever think of it again. I can't bear to believe that you were at Buchenwald and yet… poor darling, I hope that you weren't too badly treated. I will do everything to make you forget these awful things and I will take care of you with all my love and all my devotion.

I love you. Come home quickly.

Thousands and thousands of kisses

Your Irène

FIFTEEN
THE RETURN

What awaited Roland upon his return? He was lucky – that famous luck again – to be able to come back to a loving wife and to the hope of a normal family life with Irène and young son Alex. He returned home greatly debilitated, no longer the fit, sporty young man he had been when he was captured. He weighed barely 45kg and initially was unable to keep food down at all. He returned home not only outwardly changed, but also inwardly a quite different person from the young man he had been. He had seen the worst of human behaviour; he was damaged by it, for it was not only what he had endured and witnessed, but also what he had come to understand.

Roland was always aware of the effects of these experiences on his character and those of his fellow prisoners, the moral debasement that accompanied their physical and mental sufferings.

'Justice plays no part in this world,' he wrote a few days before

Roland and son Alexandre, 'Titou', in May 1945, after Roland's return to France

the liberation of the Buchenwald camp by the Americans on 11 April 1945.

Roland came back traumatised, to a traumatised country.

•

The return of the deportees was a chaotic affair. While repatriation plans had been drawn up ahead of time by the French government in exile in Algiers to organise the arrival of perhaps two and a half million returning French men and women, they did not run smoothly. They were returning as refugees – almost one million prisoners of war, along with political prisoners, racial deportees (although many of the Jews deported from France did not return[45]), forced labourers, everyone who had been deported, sent east to concentration camps – returning home to a state stripped of every resource. The Germans had taken everything: transport routes were bombed or sabotaged; raw materials; food; transport.

The provisional government, headed by General Charles de Gaulle who had built up the Free French Forces from his London base, was formally recognised in October 1944 by the US, British and Soviet governments. Henry Frenay, who was the founder of Combat, one of the main Resistance groups, was in charge of the planning at the Commissariat aux Prisonniers et Déportés. When prisoners of war started coming home at the end of the First World War – and remember that this was merely some twenty-six-plus years before – they came home accompanied by the Spanish flu. Like Covid-19 of the present day, the virus unleashed an epidemic of unmanageable and unexpected proportions. The organisers of the 1945 exodus did not want a repeat of that.

Instead of a flu epidemic, France became gripped by a crisis of recrimination and the desire for revenge. Those who had collaborated with the occupying Germans were the enemy of those who had not, of those who had fought against the occupiers. Fear of communism was widespread, the civil war in Spain fought between nationalists and

....
45 Around 2,500 Jews returned out of a total of 75,721 deported. Caroline Moorehead (2012). *A Train in Winter: A Story of Resistance, Friendship and Survival in Auschwitz.* London: Vintage. P. 293

republicans in the years leading up to the outbreak of the Second World War was hugely influential, and those politicians who survived the war justified their actions with talk of the need to guard against extreme political ideologies. Anger boiled over. There was a need, a longing for *épuration*, purification.

Some historians describe the actions aimed at holding collaborators to account that started before the liberation as the *épuration sauvage*, or non-judicial purification, so-called because it preceded the official trials under the national purge carried out according to the wishes of de Gaulle. In a study of three local purges, it is argued that there wasn't one defined purge, the *épuration sauvage*, by individuals, then another government official one, but rather people had to get to grips with their own need for justice, for revenge, to find ways to live together once more. Local purges may have acted as a means of atonement and even redemption, religious notions that informed many people's approaches to the world in what was a culturally Catholic country.[46]

However the purges are described, they were an attempt to identify and punish those who had collaborated to a greater or lesser extent with the German occupiers. The term encompasses a whole outpouring of pain, anger and bitterness from those who had suffered so much. This initial period of *épuration* was already starting in 1944 before the Normandy landings, before Roland and other deportees had come home. What were they coming home to? Who was to be punished? What did collaboration mean in an occupied country, particularly when your own government's policy from the outset had been one of collaboration? What did collaboration mean when the French police enthusiastically obeyed orders that led to the deaths and deportation of so many of their compatriots? People had to make judgements all the time about how to live, what to forgive, what they could accept both in themselves and in others. Complicity had its own scale of degrees.

Roland spent his life working for the French railways, the SNCF, la Société Nationale des Chemins de Fer, whose employees transported

....
46 The Collaborator's Penance: The Local Purge, 1944–5. Megan Koreman. *Contemporary European History*. Vol. 6, No.2 (July 1997), pp. 177-192. Cambridge University Press. https://www.jstor.org/stable/20081624

deportees on the first part of the journey towards the camps – the very same journey that Roland had made. Should the train drivers be punished?

Roland also mentions, with some disdain, those who joined the Resistance towards the end of the war, *les résistants de la dernière heure*. Was their late conversion to the cause to be celebrated or seen for what it was, a means of saving their own skin?

A French woman goes out with a German soldier, perhaps they fall in love. Does she deserve the same humiliation and punishment as the person who denounces their next-door neighbour, who is Jewish?

In Marcel Ophuls' documentary film on the Occupation, *Le Chagrin et La Pitié (The Sorrow and the Pity)*,[47] those who lived through the war and its aftermath, including a German officer, comfortably ensconced in the heart of his family, Resistance fighters, collaborators, survivors, all talk frankly of their feelings and experiences. The film sets out to examine the narrative of French Resistance and to probe into the workings of collaboration and what complicity meant for the people in occupied France, in all their diversity.

A British agent talks of his admiration for the workers, the salesgirls in the local supermarket, and everyone's willingness to help him out, to find the supplies he needed. The bourgeoisie were more frightened, he says, they had more to lose. He also talks of his love affair with a German soldier, who did not survive but was killed in Russia.

A German officer describes how the situation got worse after Germany occupied the whole of France, how people lived in terror of the German police, the Gestapo, and of the retaliation wrought upon them by the Gestapo if they resisted. A French military man with fascist beliefs talks of how many military men in France were humiliated and preferred to be on active service with the Germans on the Eastern Front, fighting the Bolsheviks. The witness joined the Charlemagne Division of the Waffen-SS, composed mainly of French volunteers fighting in German uniform for the Third Reich.

Released in 1969, the film was not broadcast on national French television until 1981. It is organised in two parts: *L'effondrement* (The

---

47 *Le Chagrin et la Pitié* (1969). Directed by Marcel Ophuls. Producers: Norddeutscher Rundfunk; Société Suisse de Radiodiffusion.

Collapse) and *Le choix* (The Choice) and is set in the Auvergne in the French industrial city of Clermont-Ferrand.

The film also includes interviews with significant public figures of the time, including Pierre Mendès-France, a Jewish politician who held office in the Popular Front government, an electoral alliance of the left, led by Léon Blum before the war. He joined the French Air Force when war broke out. Mendès-France was jailed by the Vichy government on a false accusation but escaped in 1941 and set off for Britain to join de Gaulle's Free French Forces. Anthony Eden, the British Foreign Secretary at the time, is also interviewed as a witness. Eden served as Foreign Secretary three times, the second from December 1940 until July 1945, under Prime Minister Winston Churchill, and as British Prime Minister from April 1955 until January 1957. Eden memorably said of the French experience during the war that no nation had the right to sit in judgement on another who hasn't been through it.

Every person could believe themselves tainted in some way. Collaboration for many was simply a way to survive – to be able to feed their children, to care for their families. However, some were much more tainted than others.

It was a very confused, sometimes terribly brutal period after the liberation. Not everyone admired the Resistance, seen by some as profiteers, thieves and outsiders, or feared and resented because of the reprisals carried out against ordinary people in retaliation for a Resistance action against the German occupiers; but when liberation came, the more active collaborators now found themselves at the mercy of those whom they had opposed and sometimes betrayed. Many after liberation claimed membership of the Resistance in an attempt to avoid retribution.

•

Roland's cousin Josette, daughter of his uncle Alexis, one of four sons born to Roland's paternal grandfather Pierre and his wife, along with their daughter Léa, suffered the most dramatic fate at the end of the war.

Josette had also grown up in a family sluiced in tragedy.

Roland's uncle Alexis was a qualified craftsman who worked in warship construction and maintenance in Brest. Roland describes him as a reserved man, 'experienced, conscientious, and skilled'. Alexis' wife, not named by Roland in his notes, was 'an uncritical Christian… doubtless a good mother, but I think she was quite authoritarian, and her husband stood by her out of Christian duty rather than because of love.' They had several children, but only one reached adulthood, daughter Josette. The others died as babies or very young.

Alexis died while 'in the full bloom of life' in a professional accident. A photo discovered by the family pictures him working on a destroyer.

Josette married a practising Catholic who was a Pétainist, a supporter of Vichy's head of government Marshal Pétain. Following liberation he was prosecuted probably for his pro-Vichy activities. He was shot without a trial in front of his wife. She threw herself in front of him to protect him and was killed by the shower of bullets. Her mother didn't live for very long either.

All the members of the entire family died prematurely.

•

The mood in France as the war ended was not one of jubilation. It was one of disappointment, belying the public images of a joyful relief. All those belonging to the various resistance organisations who had great hopes of creating a post-war reforming movement were badly let down as all the old patterns re-emerged. Party politicians and bureaucrats simply went back to the old familiar models of government. (Gildea, p. 444.) People returning from the camps came home more often than not to find their families torn apart and that the venal and the traitorous had not been punished.

In this respect, Roland was again 'lucky'. Not only had he survived; his family had survived. Even in his much-reduced state, he could appreciate what he had. Nevertheless, he also shared in this national disappointment. More personally, like other returning deportees, Roland may have found himself in an invidious situation. For not all of those returning to France were treated equally. In effect, there was a hierarchy of suffering.

The lines of confrontation were between Resistance fighters, prisoners of war and civilian deportees; even within these groups there were further definitions. Political deportees claimed a different status from labour deportees. Forced labourers did not put themselves in the same camp as so-called voluntary workers, in reality those conscripted by their own government into the STO. This was not exactly a voluntary act.

STO workers were reintegrated rapidly both in the workplace and socially upon their return in 1945, but French society increasingly refused to recognise these forced labourers as being the victims of either the Nazi or Pétain regimes – a situation that has continued well into the twenty-first century.[48]

Forced labourers were not properly represented for many years after the war in the collective remembrance. This is something that Jean Poulard attests to vigorously in the appendix to his translation of his brother Elie's memoir. He describes the long debate around use of the term *déporté* when applied to forced labourers. The issue has been discussed at governmental level, fought over in the courts and still to this day has not been properly resolved. Survivors of the STO are considered these days as *'victimes du travail forcé en Allemagne nazie'* (victims of forced labour in Nazi Germany), as they were not allowed to call themselves *'déportés du travail'*. Poulard argues that they were clearly deported from their home country and that there is no reason to call them anything other than *'déportés du travail'*.

In *Lendemains de Libération*,[49] a novel inspired by the writer Daniel Crozes' father's own two years as an STO worker who returned to a hostile France, a young man returns to the southern region of the Aveyron after two harsh years working in a munitions factory in Austria. In his hometown he encounters prejudice and misery. He is weak, barely able to look after himself, yet he now has to launch himself into a campaign of rehabilitation and make sense of a world where people are themselves grappling with their own loyalties, their own decisions, their own moral behaviour. (In more recent times, twenty-five or so years after the end of the Second World War, returning US soldiers from the divisive war in Vietnam also found themselves receiving less than a hero's welcome.)

In one scene, a local Catholic bishop, a defender of Pétain and Vichy, harangues the collective audience, many of them forced labourers, on the importance of forgiving their 'employers'. This is unconscionable for many, who utterly rejected the Church's assertion that the defeat was an act of God, but who instead blamed much more earthly circumstances for

---

48 Christoph Thonfeld (2011). *Memories of former World War Two forced labourers – an international comparison*. Oral History Society, Volume 39, No. 2. pp. 33–48. https://www.jstor.org/stable/41332163
49 Daniel Crozes (2017). *Lendemains de Libération*. Paris: Editions du Rouergue

France's desperate defeat, namely: lack of preparation by the armed forces and governmental incompetence. How could this bishop urge such an emollient approach after what they had suffered – and suffered with the encouragement of the Church?

Needless to say, Roland had little time for religion, despite his beloved wife Irène's own faith. 'He was an atheist,' says daughter Annie, but he never made fun of her. She does remember, however, one conversation her parents were having about death. 'Dad said that Mum should be happy to die quickly, to be with the good Lord, because she was a believer.' 'Oh no, no,' her mother protested.

'She was very religious, a Catholic, a strong believer. Her faith must have helped her when Dad was in Germany. I remember her going to church when I was taking exams.' Annie laughs about it now, how her mother would say 'a little prayer solves everything'.

'But for sure, it must have been a comfort.'

Daniel Crozes' father never told his family of what he went through, so Crozes turned to other recorded memories, including the notebooks of his uncle, an STO worker in Poland from March 1943 until January 1945. The book was only published in 2017, the year after the Poulard memoir.

The past continues to haunt us, as it should.

•

Roland never spoke of any backlash he may have suffered upon his return. And indeed, he was not conscripted under the STO laws; he was trapped in a roundup into which he had unwittingly cycled on a pleasant morning in spring. His capture led to his enforced labour, most particularly in the factory at Eisenach, but his identity papers generally refer to him as a *déporté*.

On his ID card from the Ministère des Anciens Combattants et Victimes de la Guerre (Department for Former Combatants and Victims of the War), Roland is a *déporté politique*. On another ID card, issued from the same office, he is a *combattant.* His *carte de rapatrié* (repatriation card) is issued by the Ministère des Prisonniers, Déportés et Réfugiés (Department for Prisoners, Deportees and Refugees). The local government office, la Direction Départementale de Lot-et-Garonne, also issued Roland with a certificate in Agen on 24 May 1949, attesting to his status as a *déporté politique* in Germany from 21 May 1944 until 10 May 1945.

Nevertheless, in the collective memory, the experiences of a forced labourer could not compete with those of soldiers who had suffered and died in the trenches in the First World War (which, never forget, ended barely twenty-seven years before Roland's return from Buchenwald to France). And nor could they compete with those who had been sent to the concentration camps or joined the Resistance.

Roland's experience of return may also have been ambiguous. So many others from the same roundup didn't make it home.

•

THE AFTERMATH

Those deportees who did make it home tended not to speak of their experiences. Certainly, Roland chose not to. How could he describe the degradation of his life as a forced labourer in those brutal places? And how could he explain his own survival?

He had come back to a society that had continued to function in his absence, albeit in a morally ambiguous way. People had to eat. They had to find essential supplies. People had to look after their children. They had to take care of livestock. Life had to continue. People had to do what was necessary.

In Lacapelle-Biron and its environs, with the men and boys gone, life had organised itself around the women whose tenacity and courage allowed

Irène's identity card 1944–45

the economic and social life of the community to continue, according to the keepers of the community's collective memories.

Jacques Augié's mother, for example, continued to run the family's bakery after her husband Abel was taken away. Until his capture, he had run the bakery with his thirteen-year-old son, Jacques' older brother. Their mother continued to run it single-handedly, during the next ten years. Abel died in February 1945 at Dachau, but the family was not officially informed of his death until July 1945, when they received a letter.

The priest, M Roger Dané, who was deported but who survived, was the one to give Jacques' mother the news of her husband's death. This priest had a chance to escape when the Germans offered him the choice of staying behind. He protested that it was his duty to stay with his parishioners. Before he was taken, he was a reasonably substantial man with a belly, but he returned from the camps quite skeletal. It wasn't easy to recognise him, say the witnesses.

Marie-Claire Caumières, whose father Raoul Marmié died in Dachau, remains haunted by the few memories she has of her father and by nightmares of the day the soldiers came.

'The broad outline of my dad with his cap on, leaning towards me to hug me and congratulate me on my first good mark; the same figure walking in front of me in the snow, making a narrow path with his shovel between the house and the school. And yet I didn't start school until after Easter. The snow must have arrived late in 1944.

'And there he is once again, this square figure, comforting, lifting me up from the stone staircase that I had just tumbled down, in too much of a hurry to find him in the cellar!

'And then, nothing, no more pictures, just the memory of a childhood spent waiting, hoping…

'One particular example: the memory of playing hide and seek. If I stayed put with my eyes closed for a long, long moment, that would give him time to come back and when I opened my eyes, he would be there. But at the end of the count, I was always disappointed. There was only absence, nothing but absence. I didn't know, or want to know, that everything was hopeless from the outset.

'… And always the nightmare, this famous terrible nightmare, always the same one, which haunted my feverish moments throughout the years.

The Germans were there, on my bed, on my big puffy feather eiderdown; they were there, with their boots, their helmets, their weapons, coming to get me. I watched them coming towards me, I screamed out in terror until Mum came and switched on the light which somehow had the power to vanquish the torturers.

'And even today, I still feel unease when I see a military lorry or just a gathering of men in khaki uniform.

'And always, always, the anguish I feel when for whatever reason one of my loved ones is late. The word anguish is not strong enough, it is a wave that overwhelms me, that takes over my entire being, as the minutes tick by. A fear in the pit of my stomach, a disproportionate panic that I cannot explain, nor control, nor share. It's the certainty that I will never again set eyes on the person I am waiting for.

'But also, so long afterwards, and growing stronger by the day, the refusal to accept the arbitrary, to submit blindly, a rebellious spirit, the desire to fight for the causes that I believe to be just, and the often excessive energy that I put into this fight – in brief, the love of freedom.'

•

Roland came back to a country he did not recognise. He found it hard to reintegrate into a country riven with so many different and apparently irreconcilable feelings.

Like many deportees, Roland was unwilling to talk about his experiences immediately afterwards. They had suffered arrest and deportation; they had been treated cruelly; would talking stir up too much pain? How could anyone understand if they hadn't endured such experiences themselves?

However, it wasn't simply a reluctance to share the memories. In truth, people did not want to hear about them. They were exhausted. The future had to be better. Why dwell on the horror? For some, writing down these experiences was a private way of coping with them, of ordering them, ultimately of trying to tame them. Roland composed his memoir only a few years after the events, but he continued to keep a journal throughout his life. Much later on, some twenty years after the end of the war, he writes of how much he is still affected by that time.

'Those who have lived in these materially and morally sordid places have undergone the most brutal test that can scar a man's life forever.'

As the days, months, years rolled on after that summer of 1944, the consequences of that experience became clearer in the lives of Roland and his family.

'For those who have lived through it, this period of deportation can't just become a bad memory. The physical traces left by this experience continue or grow worse; the mental traces have faded, yet remembering makes you bitter, leaves an unspeakable sense of nausea. The once uncontrollable hatred I felt for several years has lessened over time.

'Those who died, and those who survived, deserve all the sympathy of the living, but can you go on screaming for vengeance?

'The rivers renew themselves; nature changes its finery many times; and we humans are replaced by new generations. Should we demand of the young that they should take charge of our moral legacy? No, I don't think so. But they should know how to learn from our sufferings and also, it has to be said, from our mistakes.'

•

'Sometimes, he was fed up, *il avait le cafard*,' says Annie of her father. 'But I never saw Dad being depressed.' She admits, however, that he was 'disappointed'.

'Was he really unhappy in France when he came back?' I ask.

'After the war, having suffered what he suffered, he expected something else,' she says. 'That's why he left for West Africa to find a new people.'

Where he might have expected to feel some ease back in France, he felt instead that his country, or more precisely his compatriots, had failed him. And so Roland took his family and left for Africa just as his father had done before him, in the hope of a more satisfying life and a less dispiriting future. The family decamped to Sénégal first of all. Annie was born in the capital Dakar in 1947, some two years after their arrival.

'Did Irène leave family behind when they left for Sénégal?' I ask Annie.

'Oh yes, but it was such an adventure,' she says. Irène left her mother and brothers and sisters behind to join Roland on this adventure in a country that had become the heart of France's West African empire at that time. The colonists were expected to spend two years working in the country, then take six months leave back in France. The family would go back to see family in the Lot-et-Garonne region, settling in Villeneuve. Roland eventually had a house built there, which became his bolthole, his safe haven.

Roland abandoned France, but not without regret. These are his words:

'In this strange land I miss the wind of my mother country. I miss the temperate breezes. I even miss the freezing breezes coming down off the mountains. The seasons follow on from each other; nature puts on all its colours before dying, only to be reborn even fresher and more life-giving.

'Sweet France, your people are nothing like you. I have left you behind, but every day I weep for you. I miss the soft welcoming earth, the shaded sweet-smelling places, the lovely peace that I often felt as I walked along your high green banks. Where are the murmurs of the streams, the twittering of the birds in the countryside? When will I rediscover the morning damp, the fresh dawns, the fading twilights? Where have I come to lose myself?'

•

Life in Sénégal felt like a burden sometimes too. Roland writes of a general feeling of disillusion, almost of despair. His disappointment is with other human beings, wherever they are:

'In this too-hot Africa where each day I lose a little more of my vitality, where each day my health deteriorates, my strength fades. Why did I want to send myself into exile? I wanted to leave a people that disappointed me at every step, I wanted to run away from customs that wore me down at every moment. Ultimately, I wanted to run away from the temptation of wrongdoing, from the immorality, the crimes against humanity. Yes, I fled. But where did I flee to? And what have I found that would make me feel better about men, my fellow creatures? Have I found men who have not been perverted by the German occupation here in this Africa that I have overrated? Have I found this old colonial fraternity so praised by my father? Upon my arrival in this black Africa, have I found the demonstrations of mutual aid never proven wrong?

'Alas, such disillusion.'

Roland wrote that he wished he had spent more time with his uncle Gaston, learning from him about living in symbiosis with nature. Gaston lived a semi-feral life after the First World War and seemed to have suffered from shellshock. This damaged man roamed the woods and survived, even thrived, on this life in nature. He lived with his mother, who must have been a remarkably resilient woman. Roland's reasons for this regret are not what you might expect. Far from seeing his uncle's suffering during the war as an indictment of it and as offering a lesson to the future, he simply says, 'I bitterly regret not having got to know him better as the life of this woodsman might have been enlightening about the integration of life and nature.'

Gaston died quite young, around sixty. Roland's father Alexandre was present at his funeral and told the young Roland that he had returned to the village of his birth and lived there tranquilly in the same house which had been the centre of his life. Roland also sought peace and tranquillity. Like Gaston, he valued the natural world above almost everything.

In his journal, found by Annie, he writes:

'I was deprived of freedom, of every imaginable freedom for ten months. I spent my days enclosed. I could barely see the horizon. When I had the chance to get outside in the fresh air after a bombing raid, the simple fact of breathing the air, of being in nature, however inhospitable, gave me an indescribable pleasure. Just being able to see before me a horizon, an infinite landscape of fields, woods, skies, while behind me, not even a metre away, stood the guards and my fellow prisoners, gave me the impression of having rediscovered that beloved freedom whose memory can never fade.'

Roland worked for the railways, which meant there were many opportunities to travel. Irène would have loved to take advantage of these opportunities, says her daughter, but even when they retired, Roland preferred to stay at home, in his familiar house in Villeneuve, tending his familiar garden.

'Was Irène happy about that?' I ask Annie.

'She did some trips with groups, she was in a choir. She would have liked to travel with him, but because he preferred to stay at home…' Annie trails off.

It is clear that Irène and Roland had to learn to accommodate each other. Irène herself, like Gaston's mother, must have been a remarkable woman. Annie remembers them as good parents, most particularly, fair parents. She feels she had a privileged childhood, a protected childhood and is very grateful for that.

Elie Poulard found consolation and joy in his religious belief and in music, after the horrors of forced labour and separation from everything he loved and valued. Jean Hélion, the soldier turned artist, escaped from the Germans and, like Roland, made his escape from France. He fetched up in the USA and found his consolation and joy in art. For Roland, a life with some connection to the natural world brought him his consolation and joy. He could shed most of the brutalising effects of his experience, and even if a core of sorrow remained, he could contain it safely within him.

Roland didn't let the anger that he felt towards the occupying Germans, towards his captors, and even towards his fellow countrymen, fester in his soul. He was not filled by it. He looked outwards, he looked at what he had – his beloved family, nature, his garden, his full and fearless life. And he was filled with love.

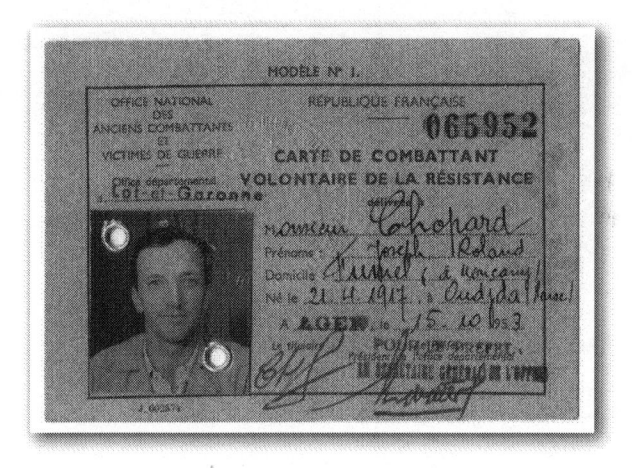

Roland's identity card, indicating his status as a former soldier and Resistance volunteer